ST/ESA/SER.A/152

Department for Economic and Social Information and Policy Analysis
Population Division

REVIEW AND APPRAISAL OF

THE WORLD POPULATION PLAN OF ACTION

1994 REPORT

United Nations
New York, 1995

NOTE

The designations employed and the presentation of the material in this report do not imply the expression of any opinion whatsoever on the part of the Secretariat of the United Nations concerning the legal status of any country, territory, city or area or of its authorities, or concerning the delimitation of its frontiers or boundaries.

The term "country" as used in the text of this report also refers, as appropriate, to territories or areas.

The report has been edited in accordance with United Nations practice and requirements.

ST/ESA/SER.A/152

UNITED NATIONS PUBLICATION

Sales No. E.95.XIII.27

ISBN 92-1-151299-9

PREFACE

The World Population Plan of Action, adopted at the World Population Conference held at Bucharest in August 1974, states that a comprehensive review and appraisal of progress made towards achieving the goals and recommendations of the Plan of Action should be taken every five years by the United Nations system. The findings of the review and appraisal should be considered by the Economic and Social Council, with the object of making appropriate modifications in the goals and recommendations of the Plan of Action. Three previous assessments were undertaken, in 1979, 1984 and 1989, by the Population Division of the Department for Economic and Social Information and Policy Analysis of the United Nations Secretariat.

The present report presents the findings of the fourth review and appraisal, focusing on 30 selected population issues. It provides an overall assessment of the level of implementation of the World Population Plan of Action and appropriate background information on population trends and policies that helped facilitate the deliberations at the International Conference on Population and Development, held in Cairo in September 1994.

Acknowledgement is due to other divisions of the Department for Economic and Social Information and Policy Analysis, the regional commissions, the United Nations Population Fund (UNFPA), the specialized agencies and other bodies and programmes of the United Nations system, and to several non-governmental organizations, for their cooperation in the preparation of the present report.

CONTENTS

TABLES

No.

Explanatory notes

Symbols of United Nations documents are composed of capital letters combined with figures.

The following symbols have been used in the tables throughout this report:

Two dots (..) indicate that data are not available or are not separately reported.

An em dash (—) indicates that the amount is nil or negligible.

A hyphen (-) indicates that the item is not applicable.

A minus sign (-) before a number indicates a decrease.

A point (.) is used to indicate decimals.

A slash (/) indicates a crop year or financial year, e.g., 1994/95.

Use of a hyphen (-) between dates representing years (e.g., 1994-1995), signifies the full period involved, including the beginning and end years.

Details and percentages in table do not necessarily add to totals because of rounding.

Reference to "dollars" ($) indicates United States dollars, unless otherwise stated.

The term "billion" signifies a thousand million.

The following abbreviations have been used in this report:

ACC	Administrative Committee on Coordination
AGFUND	Arab Gulf Programme for United Nations Development Organizations
AIDS	acquired immunodeficiency syndrome
CAPP	Computerized System for Agriculture and Population Planning and Analysis (FAO)
CELADE	Centro Latinoamericano de Demografía
CFC	chlorofluorocarbons
CPC	Committee for Programme and Coordination (United Nations)
CSN	country strategy note
DHS	Demographic and Health Survey
DISTAT	Disability Statistics Database
DOCPAL	Latin American Population Documentation System (at ECLAC)
EBIS	ESCAP Bibliographic Information System
POPFILE	Population file of ESCAP Bibliographic Information System
ECA	Economic Commission for Africa
ECE	Economic Commission for Europe
ECLAC	Economic Commission for Latin America and the Caribbean
ESCAP	Economic and Social Commission for Asia and the Pacific
ESCWA	Economic and Social Commission for Western Asia
FAO	Food and Agriculture Organization of the United Nations
HIV	human immunodeficiency virus
IACC	Inter-Agency Consultative Committee (UNFPA)
IDA	International Development Association
IEC	information, education and communication
IFAD	International Fund for Agricultural Development
IIEP	International Environmental Education Programme
ILO	International Labour Organization
IOM	International Organization for Migration
INSTRAW	International Research and Training Institute for the Advancement of Women

IPALCA	Information Network on Population for Latin America and the Caribbean
IPPF	International Planned Parenthood Federation
IRCA	Immigration Reform and Control Act (United States)
IUSSP	International Union for the Scientific Study of Population
JCGP	Joint Consultative Group on Policy (UNFPA)
MCH/FP	maternal and child health/family planning
NHSCP	National Household Survey Capability Programme
OAU	Organization of African Unity
OECD	Organization for Economic Co-operation and Development
PAPCHILD	Pan-Arab Project for Child Development
POPIN	Population Information Network (United Nations)
PRSD	Programme Review and Strategy Development (UNFPA)
SEADE	Fundação Sistema Estadual de Analise de Dados
TCDC	technical cooperation among developing countries
TSS	technical support system (UNFPA)
UNCED	United Nations Conference on Environment and Development
UNCTAD	United Nations Conference on Trade and Development
UNDP	United Nations Development Programme
UNEP	United Nations Environment Programme
UNESCO	United Nations Educational, Scientific and Cultural Organization
UNFPA	United Nations Population Fund
UNHCR	Office of the United Nations High Commissioner for Refugees
UNICEF	United Nations Children's Fund
UNIDO	United Nations Industrial Development Organization
UNITWIN	UNESCO twinning arrangements projects
UNRWA	United Nations Relief and Works Agency for Palestine Refugees in the Near East
USAID	United States Agency for International Development
WFP	World Food Programme
WFS	World Fertility Survey
WISTAT	Women's Indicators and Statistics Database
WHO	World Health Organization
WMO	World Meteorological Organization

INTRODUCTION

1. The World Population Plan of Action (United Nations, 1975) which was adopted by the United Nations World Population Conference, held at Bucharest in 1974, stipulates (para. 108) that a comprehensive and thorough review and appraisal of progress made towards achieving the goals and recommendations of the Plan of Action should be undertaken every five years by the United Nations system. In order to make appropriate modifications to the goals and recommendations, the Economic and Social Council considered the three previous reviews and appraisals, undertaken in 1979, 1984 and 1989 (United Nations, 1979, 1986, and 1989b, respectively), and adopted a total of 117 additional recommendations for the further implementation of the Plan of Action. The findings of the second assessment— discussed at the International Conference on Population, held at Mexico City in 1984—provided the rationale for a set of 88 recommendations which hereinafter will be referred to as the Mexico City recommendations (United Nations, 1984).

2. Normally, the present report would have covered the findings of the fourth review and appraisal only, for the period 1989-1994. However, considering that a new programme of action was expected to be adopted at the International Conference on Population and Development, to be held in Cairo in 1994, it was deemed more appropriate for this report to cover the entire period following the adoption of the Plan of Action in 1974. However, this present report also takes into account the general debate which took place in Cairo and makes reference to the Programme of Action adopted there. The appropriate background information on trends and policies provided by this report, as well as the illustration of the major advances and successes in applying the provisions of the Plan of Action, the lessons learned and issues that have emerged, were intended to facilitate the deliberations of the International Conference on Population and Development.

3. At its twenty-fifth session, the Population Commission suggested that the fourth review and appraisal should concentrate on a selected number of issues, as was done in the third assessment (United Nations, 1989b). As a result of various consultations, including a discussion with the members of the inter-agency task force established for the Conference by the Administrative Committee on Coordination (ACC), 31 issues were selected (United Nations, 1992a and 1993a).

4. The present report covers the major topics of the Plan of Action, but follows the structure of the Programme of Action of the 1994 Conference. The structure of the two documents might be better understood if the proposed actions are grouped in three major sets, as follows:

(a) Areas that are the subject-matter of the Plan of Action: namely, socio-economic development and population; women; the family; and the major demographic factors—namely, population growth and demographic structures, human reproduction, mortality, population distribution, and internal and international migration (chaps. I-IX and XV below);

(b) Planned activities that will affect the subject areas presented in the first set: data collection and analysis, research, provision of services, managerial operations of programmes, creation of awareness, and information, education and communication activities, and evaluation of actions (chaps. X and XI);

(c) Different actors that are responsible for the activities in each area: Governments; the international community; non-governmental organizations; the private sector; scholars; and the media, among others (chaps. XII-XIV). For each of the topics included in the present report, there is a brief summary of overall trends and tendencies, a description of the most salient issues related to the topic, indicating its relevance, actions contemplated by the Plan of Action (if any), measures adopted by Governments and by the international community, and an assessment of the implementation of the Plan of Action.

5. For the preparation of the report, a large number of sources were used. Among the most important were the preparatory activities for the 1994 Conference (namely, the documentation for the six expert group meetings and the five regional population conferences and the deliberations of the Preparatory Committee for the Conference), and the products of various activities in the work programme of relevant units of the United Nations system, such as the results of the 1991 and the 1993 biennial reports on the monitoring of population trends and policies (United Nations, 1992b, and forthcoming, respectively); the report of the Secretary-General on monitoring of multilateral population assistance (E/CN.9/1994/6); the reports of the Secretary-General on the activities of the United Nations system in the field of population (E/CN.9/1994/5) and on the work of intergovernmental and non-governmental organizations in the implementation of the World Population Plan of Action (E/CN.9/1994/7), and information from the Population Policy Data Bank maintained by the Population Division of the Department for Economic and Social Information and Policy Analysis of the United Nations Secretariat (hereinafter referred to as the Population Policy Data Bank), which also includes the findings of the seven Population Inquiries among Governments.

6. The present review, like the three previous reviews, has been carried out by the relevant units of the United Nations system. Owing to stringent budgetary constraints, it was conducted with the utmost economy of resources, by making extensive use of existing facilities and coordinating mechanisms, as recommended by the Population Commission. The report has been prepared by the Population Division of the Department for Economic and Social Information and Policy Analysis of the United Nations Secretariat, with valuable contributions from other divisions of the same Department, the regional commissions, the United Nations Population Fund (UNFPA), the specialized agencies and other bodies and programmes of the United Nations system, and several non-governmental organizations. The views expressed on the review and appraisal at the International Conference on Population and Development (United Nations, 1994b) have been incorporated into the present report.

I. PRINCIPLES AND OBJECTIVES OF THE WORLD POPULATION PLAN OF ACTION

7. The World Population Plan of Action contains a list of principles and objectives which set forth the rationale for action in the field of population and the guiding criteria and expected results of such action (paras. 14-15). They may be perceived as constituting the structural segment of the Plan, while the recommendations that follow constitute the instruments to be used in order to achieve its objectives. The three previous reviews and appraisals have shown that the validity of the principles and objectives are universally recognized by national Governments, the international community and non-governmental organizations. The Economic and Social Council, in its resolution 1981/87 on the convening of the International Conference on Population in 1984, decided that the 1984 Conference should work within the framework of the existing World Population Plan of Action, the principles and objectives of which continued to be fully valid.

Issue No. 1. Individual rights and responsibilities
versus societal goals and objectives

8. During the deliberations at the first and second sessions of the Preparatory Committee for the International Conference on Population and Development, and at various sessions of the Economic and Social Council, it was suggested that the relationships between individual rights and societal goals be discussed, inasmuch as certain specific situations might create ambiguities in the way human rights were recognized and respected. Although the Plan of Action affirms (para. 14) that the formulation and implementation of population policies is the sovereign right of each nation, it also states that all couples and individuals have the basic right to decide freely and responsibly the number and spacing of their children and to have the information, education and means to do so (para. 14 (*f*)). Individual rights and societal goals may be at odds in some specific circumstances, particularly in periods of rapid social change. Human reproduction and other demographic phenomena are not so very different from other elements of the reality of social life, where in many instances individuals, whatever their rights, face strong appeals to conform to societal goals. The Plan of Action, however, clearly recommends (para. 29 (*a*)) that all countries should respect and ensure, regardless of their overall demographic goals, the right of persons to determine, in a free, informed and responsible manner, the number and spacing of their children. The Plan of Action also acknowledges (para. 34) that family size may also be affected by incentives and disincentive schemes, but it emphasizes that if such schemes are adopted or modified, it is essential that they should not violate human rights. The Plan of Action rejects any form of coercion.

3

9.   The principle that couples and individuals have the basic right to decide freely and responsibly the number and spacing of their children (para. 14 (*f*) of the Plan of Action) also stipulates that the responsibility of couples and individuals in the exercise of this right takes into account the needs of their living and future children, and their responsibilities towards the community. Such consideration of the needs and rights of future generations is precisely at the core of the concept of sustainable development. It is also consistent with the widely recognized notion that rights, entail obligations and that responsibilities apply to duties not only *vis-à-vis* other human beings but also *vis-à-vis* future generations. In the Mexico City recommendations it was affirmed (recommendation 24, para. 26) that experience since the adoption of the Plan of Action had suggested that Governments could do more to assist people in making their reproductive decisions in a responsible way. This statement is still applicable and is relevant to the trends observed in the present decade. Lastly, the importance of considering both individual rights and responsibilities and societal goals and obligations, while addressing the various aspects of population and sustainable development issues, was acknowledged in the Principles set forth in the Programme of Action adopted by the International Conference on Population and Development.

II. SOCIO-ECONOMIC DEVELOPMENT, THE ENVIRONMENT AND POPULATION

10. The explicit aim of the World Population Plan of Action is to help coordinate population trends and the trends of economic and social development (para. 1). Population policies and programmes are conceived by the Plan of Action as constituent elements of socio-economic development policies (para. 14 (*d*)) whose aim is to affect, *inter alia*, population growth, morbidity and mortality, reproduction and family formation, population distribution and internal migration, international migration and, consequently, demographic structures (para. 15 (*c*)). The two issues discussed below were selected to illustrate the level of implementation of the Plan of Action in terms of the socio-economic transformation proposed by the Plan and the interrelationships between population, the environment and the process of development.

Issue No. 2.   Population and socio-economic development

11. The Plan of Action affirms, as one of its principles, that population and development are interrelated (para 14 (*c*)). To meet the challenges of development, in the Plan of Action (paras. 68-70) and the Mexico City recommendations (para. 14 and particularly recommendations 1-3), adopted at the International Conference on Population in 1984, Governments are urged to adopt an integrated approach to population and development, both in national policies and at the international level. Such recommendations also reflect the view that, although the actions of developing countries are of primary importance, the attainment of development goals will require appropriate policies and support by the developed countries and the international community.

12. The Plan of Action emphasizes that the basis for an effective solution of population problems is, above all, socio-economic transformation (para. 1). Consequently, the Plan of Action makes a number of recommendations dealing with socio-economic policies and mentions specifically certain issues, for example, development assistance, economic growth, food and agriculture, education, health and employment, with the understanding that such socio-economic transformation will modify demographic variables by creating new conditions. The wide range of issues mentioned by the Plan of Action correspond, *mutatis mutandis*, to the themes included in the past three international development strategies adopted by the General Assembly.[1] The major findings of this review and appraisal confirm, in general, the results of the previous assessments, which have concluded that the impact of economic growth on the levels of fertility and mortality is likely to be less direct than on other dimensions of development. In other words, there is increasing evidence that the resolution of demographic issues is to be found in the synergistic combination of various strategic dimensions that call for

simultaneous action on various fronts: income distribution; improvement in the status of women; gender equality; basic education; primary health care (including family planning); and employment opportunities (United Nations, 1986).

Economic growth

13.   Sustained economic growth remains an urgently important imperative throughout the developing world. Without the benefits of such growth, developing countries will not be able to improve the standards of living of their people, and a durable resolution to demographic issues will be seriously hampered. In the Declaration on International Economic Cooperation, in particular the Revitalization of Economic Growth and Development of the Developing Countries, the States Members of the United Nations strongly affirmed the need to revitalize growth and development in the developing countries and to address together the problems of abject poverty and hunger.[2] Similar ideas appear in the Declaration on the Right to Development.[3]

14.   During the past decades, the developing world has made enormous economic progress. This can be seen most clearly in the rising trend for incomes and consumption: between 1965 and 1985, consumption per capita in the developing world went up by almost 70 per cent. Other measures of well-being confirm this picture: life expectancy, infant and child mortality, and educational attainment have all improved markedly. Nevertheless, markedly diverging regional and national trends can be observed. In some areas efforts were quite successful, while in others a sequence of difficulties emerged. The very diverse trends in the growth of output per person highlight this fact.

15.   Slow growth of per capita output in Africa, at an average annual rate of 0.4 per cent in the first decade after the adoption of the Plan of Action, gave way to an outright decline of 0.6 per cent per annum after 1984. In the smaller and generally poorer countries of sub-Saharan Africa (that is, those excluding Nigeria), the situation was more extreme: an average annual decline of 1.0 per cent in the first 10 years became an average decline of 1.8 per cent per annum after 1984. In Latin America, the 1980s are commonly referred to as the "lost decade". Indeed, after per capita output rose 0.7 per cent per annum on average in the 10 years up to 1984, it has been virtually stagnating since, with a growth per capita of only 0.2 per cent per annum. Unlike the situation in Africa, however, there are now signs that growth in Latin America is on the verge of significant improvement, as economic recovery seems to have begun recently to take hold in some countries and foreign and domestic investors have brought considerable sums of foreign exchange back into the region. In other words, Latin America seems to be at a turning-point. In the Asian and Pacific region, in contrast, per capita output rose by a robust 2.6 per cent annually in the 10 years after the United Nations World Population Conference in Bucharest, and it has been rising by an even stronger 3.1 per cent per annum in the more recent period. Since the developing countries of Asia and the Pacific constitute over 70 per cent of the population living in the less developed regions, this trend is particu-

larly heartening—even more so because the more rapidly growing countries include some of the poorest of the world. In the West Asian subregion, however, output per capita has been falling 3.1 per cent per annum since 1984. While many of the citizens of this region have been fortunate to be living over vast pools of petroleum resources, they have also been afflicted by almost a decade of warfare which took an economic as well as human toll. The region is not unique in this regard. The recent devastation in the former Yugoslavia has virtually wiped out all the growth in average output per capita in the Mediterranean region since 1974.

16.   Given the important economic achievements realized by the developing countries as a group, it is all the more appalling that almost one third of the total population, or more than 1 billion people, in the developing world are still living in poverty. Progress in raising average incomes, however welcome, must not distract attention from this massive and continuing burden of poverty, which is spread unevenly among the regions of the developing world, among countries within those regions, and among localities within those countries. In countries that have exhibited a marked economic progress since the 1960s, poverty has declined and even the incomes of those remaining in poverty have increased. However, the conditions of the poor were exacerbated in countries that experienced poor economic performance. Nearly half of the world's poor live in South Asia, a region that accounts for 30 per cent of world population. Sub-Saharan Africa accounts for a smaller but still highly disproportionate share of global poverty. Poverty is usually coexistent with illiteracy, unemployment, malnutrition, poor health, low status of women and deteriorating environmental conditions. Such situations are also often accompanied by high levels of fertility, morbidity and mortality. In such cases, extensive poverty aggravates the negative impacts of population pressure on land use and, in turn, constitutes a major obstacle to obtaining fertility and mortality declines in rural areas.

17.   During the 1980s, many developing countries had to cope with economic crises and embarked on macroeconomic reforms, including stabilization policies aimed at reducing inflation and external deficits and structural adjustment programmes addressing internal and external imbalances in resource allocation in specific sectors such as trade, finance and industry. Such policies were intended to eliminate rigidities in the countries concerned and to foster a macroeconomic environment conducive to sustained economic growth. Although it is expected that in the longer term economic restructuring associated with adjustment is likely to bring about an improvement in the standard of living of the entire population, in the short term those economic policies have tended to increase the number of the poor and have put many of the poor at risk. A comparison of the experiences in various developing countries suggests that poverty reduction can be achieved by first pursuing a strategy that promotes the productive use of the poor's most abundant asset— namely, labour—in both industry and agriculture. Experience also shows that the provision of basic social services to the poor, including health care, family planning, nutrition and primary education, is equally critical.

18.   Several lessons are embedded in the above considerations. One is that peace and a functioning civil society are prerequisites of sustained eco-

nomic growth and sustainable development. A second is that rigid economic structures and excessive dependence on a limited range of commodity exports and on a thin layer of "human capital" have been extremely costly. High levels of domestic savings, access to modern technologies, low levels of inflation and, particularly, heavy investments in education have been associated with the successful case-stories. Indeed, international cooperation during this period has increasingly focused on facilitating and hastening structural adjustment and on building capacities to identify and capture opportunities. Finally, it should be repeated that poverty is increasingly recognized to be closely associated with both undesirable demographic trends and environmental degradation. Together with social and economic inequality, poverty is exacerbating and is exacerbated by the problems derived from rapid population growth. There is little doubt that economic growth is necessary to combat poverty and to provide the means to satisfy basic needs, but economic growth should be reconcilable with sustainable development. Such development may be achieved if appropriate technologies are developed and made available to developing countries on preferential and concessional terms and if suitable strategies and policies are adopted to stimulate conservation of non-renewable natural resources and avert environmental degradation.

Food and agriculture

19. The Plan of Action recognizes the important role that food and agriculture play in improving the standards of living of people and recommends that Governments give high priority to improving methods of food production, the investigation and development of new sources of food and more effective utilization of existing sources (para. 70) in response to the needs of the rapidly growing world population. Trends in per capita food production and food supplies have, to a large extent, paralleled trends in per capita output. Such a situation is not very different from the one assessed a decade ago when the second review and appraisal found that, globally, the growth of food production had more than kept pace with the rate of population increase and was projected to do so in the future (United Nations, 1986). Similar findings were noted in the third review and appraisal (United Nations, 1989b). Equally remarkable is the fact that during the past three decades the number of countries that have been able to meet their daily per capita requirements has gone from less than 25 to more than 50. Nevertheless, enormous disparities account for the fact that about 800 million people still do not get sufficient food.[4]

20. During the 1980s, per capita food production continued to grow at the global level. At the world level, the average food production per capita increased 1.1 per cent per annum on average. This growth took place mostly in the developing countries, reflecting above all high growth rates in Asia (China and India increased their production by 27 per cent during the periods 1979-1981 and 1988-1990). Sub-Saharan Africa continued on its long-term path to decline (minus 0.5 per cent per annum). Per capita food supplies continued to increase at the global level, but there was no progress in sub-

8

Saharan Africa (with per capita food supplies stagnant at grossly inadequate levels) or Latin America.

21. The overall incidence of undernutrition declined significantly in relative terms but only slightly in absolute terms in the developing countries. However, the incidence of undernutrition increased in both absolute and relative terms in sub-Saharan Africa and in absolute terms in Latin America. The cereals deficit of the developing countries continued to increase but at a much slower rate than in the 1970s. Much of the increase originated in the growth of cereal imports into the regions of Northern Africa and Western Asia. At the global level, the Food and Agriculture Organization of the United Nations (FAO) estimates that the daily calorie supply per capita increased from 2,383 in 1965 to 2,580 in 1979-1981 and to 2,700 in 1988-1990. Important improvements have been achieved in Asia but not in Latin America, which remained stagnant at a daily calorie supply per capita of 2,690 during the past decade, or in sub-Saharan Africa, where there was a decline from 2, 120 to 2,100.

Education

22. The Plan of Action recalls the important place of education in achieving social and economic development (para. 69). Notable improvements have been registered in this area. During the past two decades, primary school enrolment increased from less than 70 to more than 80 per cent, while secondary school enrolment almost doubled, from 25 to 40 per cent. These achievements have been realized during the past decade in particular and in those countries that have guaranteed the right to education for all. The countries that have invested more in education are also those that have generally manifested a better performance in terms of economic growth, reduction of poverty and overall improvement in the standard of living of their populations. Approximately 1 billion school-age children are currently enrolled. However, sub-Saharan Africa, and Western and Southern Asia still lack sufficient school space to enrol all children in first-level education. Contrary to other developing regions, the primary school-age population in sub-Saharan Africa declined appreciably, from 79 to 67 per cent. In 1990 there were an estimated 130 million out-of-school youth in the age group 6-11 in the developing countries, and 277 million in the age group 12-17. Millions more satisfy the attendance requirements but fail to complete basic education programmes and, consequently, do not acquire essential knowledge and skills.

23. Even though the total number of illiterate adults in the world—948 million in 1990—is still important, significant progress towards adult literacy has been achieved. The adult literacy rates in all regions of the world are rising, and the global rate is expected to go above 75 per cent before the end of the century. In sub-Saharan Africa and Southern Asia the rate is expected to be lower, and a figure of 49 per cent is projected for the group of least developed countries.

24. In a majority of developing countries, girls are still underrepresented in enrolment at every level of formal education. Moreover, the opportunities for girls to advance beyond the first level of formal education to the

second and third levels are still significantly fewer than for boys. The United Nations Educational, Scientific and Cultural Organization (UNESCO) estimates that currently one out of three adult females in the world is illiterate, compared with only one out of five adult males. While there has been substantial progress in reducing male/female disparities in illiteracy, the gender differences remain pronounced in certain regions, notably Southern and Western Asia, and sub-Saharan Africa.

Health

25. Although specific aspects related to the health sector are covered in chapter VII below, it is important to mention that in general there has been notable progress in improving the health conditions of populations. However, there is still a wide gap between the health coverage of urban areas and that of rural ones. The health-care systems in the majority of the developing countries have not been able to attend properly to the needs of rural areas and have demonstrated increasing difficulties in coping with the rapidly increasing demand of fast-growing populations in the urban and suburban areas. As a result, increasing numbers of people are not receiving appropriate or comprehensive health care. Even more alarming is the gap between population growth and the amount of health-sector investments, which are even shrinking in many countries. According to the World Health Organization (WHO), this deterioration has been a result of the low priority given to the health sector by many Governments as well as of the effect on the social sector of the debt crisis and the effect of poorly designed structural adjustment policies. Furthermore, the quality of the services has become increasingly difficult to maintain or improve, since the physical infrastructure is decaying.

26. World food production outweighs consumption, as has been mentioned above. Nevertheless, the lack of access to food has affected a large number of people. Among the victims are more than 2 billion people who suffer from micronutrient deficiencies which can lead to blindness, mental retardation and death. Moreover, more than 150 million people in Asia and about 30 million people in Africa (including a large proportion of children under five years of age) suffer from protein-energy malnutrition.

Employment

27. The Plan of Action recognizes that a major challenge faced by developing countries is the creation of sufficient employment opportunities in the modern sector of their economies to absorb their rapidly growing labour force. As the six-billionth inhabitant is currently expected to be born in the year 1998, one year sooner than was projected in the late 1980s, population growth and concomitant growth in the labour force are making the employment issue a great challenge. This is especially the case for developing countries in which unemployment, underemployment and poverty are associated with low levels of investment and where the economic climate is most likely to remain unfavourable.

28. According to the International Labour Organization (ILO), the major economic factors and policies that have aggravated the employment problem are:

(a) The disproportionate emphasis given by countries to growth-oriented development strategies at the expense of other major goals;

(b) The selection of ill-suited production techniques that are capital-intensive in the industrial as well as in the agriculture sectors;

(c) The lack of an adequate balance between national production destined for export and that destined for domestic consumption;

(d) Labour-market segmentation, giving preference to capital-intensive production methods rather than to the informal sector;

(e) The insufficient monitoring of structural adjustment programmes and other policies implemented to deregulate the economy and to reduce the size of the public sector.

29. Strategies for responding adequately to the above problems have been fostered by the international community and are based on the recognition of the existing links among population growth, employment, income distribution and poverty. Such strategies aim at promoting employment in all sectors, facilitating the access to productive inputs and improved technologies, and establishing/strengthening education and training systems responding to specific employment situations.

Issue No. 3. Population and the environment

30. One of the objectives of the World Population Plan of Action is to advance national and international understanding of the complex relations among the problems of population, resources, environment and development, and to promote a unified analytical approach to the study of these interrelationships and to relevant policies (para. 15 (d)). The Plan of Action explicitly affirms that in the democratic formulation of national population goals and policies, consideration must be given, together with other economic and social factors, to the supplies and characteristics of natural resources and to the quality of the environment (para. 14 (j)). The continuing debate over the connection between population growth, development and environmental impacts has been a major concern of the international community since the 1974 World Population Conference in Bucharest. Recommendation 4 of the Mexico City Conference urged Governments to adopt and implement specific policies, including population policies, that would contribute to redressing imbalances between trends in population growth and resources and environmental requirements and promote improved methods of identifying, extracting, renewing, utilizing and conserving natural resources.

31. A major impetus to the current concern about the linkages between population factors and the environment was given by the publication in 1987 of the report of the World Commission on Environment and Development, popularly known as the Brundtland Commission (World Commission on Environment and Development, 1987), whose perhaps most important message was the introduction of the concept of sustainable development. The report

observed that rapidly growing populations could increase the pressure on resources and slow any rise in living standards. It concluded that sustainable development could only be achieved if population size and growth were in harmony with the changing productive potential of the ecosystem.

32. Two years later, in November 1989, the International Forum on Population in the Twenty-first Century adopted the Amsterdam Declaration on A Better Life for Future Generations (UNFPA, 1990). It acknowledged, *inter alia*, that population, resources and the environment were inextricably linked and stressed the commitment of the Forum's participants to bringing about a sustainable relationship between human numbers, resources and development (preamble, para. 1).

33. In 1990, the report of the South Commission (1990) acknowledged that in several developing countries, the pressure of growing numbers on the limited fertile land was accelerating the degradation of land and water resources and causing excessive deforestation. The Commission found that the current trends in population, if not moderated, had frightening implications for the ability of the South to meet the twin challenges of development and environmental security in the twenty-first century.

34. Agenda 21 (United Nations, 1993b), adopted in 1992 by the United Nations Conference on Environment and Development, recognizes that demographic trends and factors and sustainable development have a synergistic relationship, and reiterates that the growth of world population and production, combined with unsustainable consumption patterns, places increasingly severe stress on the life-supporting capacities of the planet. The pivotal contribution of the United Nations Conference on Environment and Development was its strong emphasis on the cross-sectoral linkages between issues of development and the environment. Among other important matters, it addressed the connection between demographic dynamics and sustainability, thereby extending and reinforcing the earlier references in the World Population Plan of Action and the recommendations for its further implementation. In chapter 5 of Agenda 21, five key objectives are identified within the main programme areas:

(a) To incorporate demographic trends and factors in the global analysis of environment and development issues;

(b) To develop a better understanding of the relationships among demographic dynamics, technology, cultural behaviour, natural resources and life support systems;

(c) To assess human vulnerability in ecologically sensitive areas and centres of population to determine the priorities for action at all levels;

(d) To fully integrate population concerns into national planning, policy- and decision-making processes, with full recognition of women's rights;

(e) To implement population programmes along with natural resource management and development programmes at the local level to ensure sustainable use of natural resources, improve the quality of life of the people and enhance environmental quality (United Nations, 1993).

Agenda 21 calls for developing and disseminating knowledge concerning the links between demographic trends and factors and sustainable development and, on this basis, for formulating integrated national policies and local programmes for population, the environment and development.

35. Population, development and environmental issues are linked in complex ways. The ecological impacts of population factors are shaped by the characteristics of the physical environment, as well as by the type of social organization (which includes a complex set of cultural values that determines patterns of consumption), the level of economic development and the available technological options. If the prospects for future generations are not to be compromised, important changes must be made towards the adoption of a sustainable pattern of development, one that maintains a balance between population size and environmental capacities and also succeeds in lightening the grinding burden of poverty that afflicts a large portion of the world population. A large amount of research has been done on each of the three components—population, the environment and the process of development—but of particular interest is the proper understanding of the interrelations among them. Brief illustrations of some of the linkages among population, the environment and socio-economic development are presented below.

Land use and deforestation

36. The state of the environment in rural areas is of particular importance since such areas are currently inhabited by two thirds of the population of developing countries. In areas where agriculture remains the major economic activity of increasing numbers of poor people, individuals have resorted to putting at risk the basis for further production. In particular, the growth of rural populations plays an important role in the process of deforestation through the clearing of land on the margins of tropical forest and through the quest for firewood. In the early 1980s, it was estimated that tropical deforestation was proceeding at a rate of 11.4 million hectares per annum. Recent estimates have pushed the rate up from 17 million to 20 million hectares per annum in the late 1980s. The latest statistics suggest that the overall rate of tropical deforestation in the 1980s was 0.9 per cent per annum. About 1.3 billion people live in areas where fuelwood is consumed faster than trees can regrow.

37. Population pressure on land resources also leads to fragmentation of landholdings, shortening of fallow periods, and cultivation of erosion-prone hillsides, all of which contribute to soil degradation. The phenomenon of landlessness is also widespread; the proportion of agricultural landless households is estimated to be 17 per cent in Latin America, 11 per cent in Western Asia, 15 per cent in Southern Asia and 6.5 per cent in Africa. Even more important is the proportion of smallholder households, whose landholdings are too small to provide a sustainable livelihood, with the proportion being about 60 per cent in the developing countries as a group. Under the norms of partible inheritance of land that are typical for most developing countries, rapid population growth contributes in a significant way to the fragmentation of agricultural holdings. To the extent that land fragmentation is not matched by the introduction of intensive and environmentally sustainable agricultural techniques, the farmers with exceedingly small plots are forced to "mine" their

land or migrate and engage in ecologically destructive practices of land extensification on marginal lands where soil and climatic conditions are poorly suited to annual cropping. As a result of rapid population growth, combined with the aforementioned institutional factors and lack of development, some 7 million to 8 million hectares of rain-fed croplands and 1.5 million hectares of irrigated land are currently lost every year, while another 20 million hectares lose virtually all their agricultural productivity. Rapid population growth has also been identified as one of the factors contributing to the excessive exploitation of pastures, destruction of vegetation on mountain slopes, siltation of rivers and increasing incidence of floods.

Water resources

38. With a growing world population, increased urbanization and a continuing process of economic growth, freshwater scarcity is rapidly becoming a common phenomenon. Currently, 80 countries, with 40 per cent of the world population, suffer from serious water shortages. Given existing climatic conditions and current population projections, it is estimated that the per capital global water-supply will decline by 24 per cent by the end of the twentieth century. Projections made by hydrologists indicate that meeting demands by the year 2000 will require virtually all the useable freshwater supplies in Northern Africa and Western Asia. As a result, 15-25 Northern African and sub-Saharan African countries might face serious problems with water shortages by the year 2025.

39. It is also anticipated that the projected high rates of population growth in urban areas will bring with them a rapid rate of growth in the demand for water for domestic, municipal and industrial uses. It is likely that this will further strain existing water-supply capabilities, and that the provision of additional supplies will often require the development of costlier sources. In addition, it is likely that the demand for water for urban use will compete increasingly with the growing demands of irrigation for agriculture.

40. Water shortages are further compounded by the fact that, in a number of countries, much of the available water is not safe to drink. This issue is addressed in the 1991 report of the Secretary-General to the Committee on Natural Resources at its twelfth session, on strategies and measures for the implementation of the Mar del Plata Action Plan in the 1990s (E/C.7/1991/8).

41. Thus, despite dramatic improvements in the standards and levels of services in drinking water–supply and sanitation achieved in the past two decades, especially in the rural areas of developing countries, as of 1990, 1.2 billion people did not have access to clean water-supplies, and 1.7 billion people were not served by adequate sanitary facilities. The problems of the urban environment are becoming increasingly important, given the rapid pace of the urbanization process in many developed and developing countries. Many cities have not been able to expand their infrastructures rapidly enough to cope with the environmental requirements of their burgeoning populations. In addition to the problems related to water-supply, sanitation and waste-water treatment, the disposal of solid wastes is another major en-

vironmental problem facing cities. Most settlements in Africa and Asia, including many cities with 1 million or more inhabitants, have neither sewerage systems nor refuse-collection systems. An estimated 30-50 per cent of solid wastes generated within cities is left uncollected, and 90 per cent of the sewage that is collected is discharged without treatment, thereby polluting the area's water and soil. According to a recent assessment, improvements in water-supplies and sanitation can bring a median reduction of 22 per cent in morbidity from diarrhoea (which causes about 900 million incidents of illness each year), a 28 per cent reduction in morbidity from roundworm infection (which afflicts 900 million people at any one time) and a 73 per cent reduction in morbidity from schistosomiasis (which afflicts 200 million people).

42.   Both issues of water shortages and sanitation were addressed in the report of the Secretary-General to the General Assembly at its forty-fifth session, concerning the achievements of the International Drinking Water Supply and Sanitation Decade, 1981-1990 (A/45/327). The findings of the report indicated that, in spite of the progress achieved concerning service coverage during that period, the situation in the urban areas of developing countries, particularly in large cities, could become alarming in the future. Given the high rate of growth in urban centres, the number of individuals in urban areas without adequate water-supply facilities could increase by as much as 83 per cent, and the number of dwellers without adequate sanitation services, by as much as 68 per cent. As a result, there could be a vast number of urban and rural poor lacking suitable water-supply and sanitation services and increasingly vulnerable to water-borne diseases. Finally, it appears that too often water resources projects that have been set up to address those issues have failed to benefit the urban and rural poor.

43.   Given those considerations, both the 1992 United Nations Conference on Environment and Development (UNCED), in its Agenda 21 (chap. 8), and the International Conference on Water and the Environment (World Meteorological Organization, 1992), which was convened as part of the preparatory process for UNCED, stressed, *inter alia*, the need for a holistic approach to water resources development and management, including the interrelationship between land and water, and the efficient use of those resources through demand management; the need for a participatory approach to development through management at the lowest appropriate level; the need for the use of appropriate technologies; and, lastly, the need for capacity-building. These recommendations can be seen as a further expansion of the recommendations in the 1974 World Population Plan of Action regarding the need to view the issues of development, population and the environment in a holistic manner.

Atmospheric pollution

44.   Atmospheric pollution remains an important health hazard for urban populations throughout the world. The United Nations Environment Programme (UNEP) Global Environment Monitoring System estimates that nearly 900 million urban dwellers, mostly in developing countries, are ex-

posed to unhealthy levels of sulphur dioxide and that more than 1 billion people are exposed to excessive levels of particulates. National trends in emissions and concentrations of these substances are mixed. While significant progress was made in the past two decades by countries of the Organisation for Economic Cooperation and Development (OECD), there has been little or no improvement at all in the heavily polluted industrial areas of Eastern Europe and the former Union of Soviet Socialist Republics, and in the developing countries the typical trend is towards a rise in air pollution. Environmental conditions are particularly precarious in overcrowded slums and squatter settlements which are home to an estimated 25-50 per cent of the urban population of developing countries. The use of chlorofluorocarbons (CFCs) and other ozone-depleting substances to meet the growing demand for certain consumer goods associated with the styles of the modern industrial society also has implications for the habitability of the planet and demands the adoption of strict measures.

Energy resources

45. In some respects, the situation concerning energy is similar to that concerning water resources. The growth of urban centres and increased requirements for industrial production translate themselves into growing demands for energy resources. At the same time, however, the urban and rural poor continue to suffer from inadequate sources and in many developing countries rely on fuelwood for most of their requirements. As indicated in paragraph 9.9 of Agenda 21, much of the world's energy is currently produced and consumed in ways that could not be sustained if technology were to remain constant and if overall quantities were to increase substantially. It is further pointed out that the need to control atmospheric emissions of greenhouse and other gases and substances will increasingly need to be based on efficiency in energy production. Agenda 21 calls, *inter alia*, for the identification of economically viable and environmentally sound energy sources; for the formulation of energy policies integrating economic and environmental considerations; for the promotion of the research, development, transfer and use of improved energy-efficient technologies, including new and renewable sources of energy; and for the promotion of capacity-building.

46. With regard to rural energy, the General Assembly, in its resolution 41/170, urged that greater attention be given to the development of new and renewable sources of energy for the rural sector and to their integration into the overall rural economy, bearing in mind the depletion of the fuelwood supply taking place in many regions of the world. Chapter 14 of Agenda 21 calls for the promotion of a mix of cost-effective fossil and renewable energy resources that is sustainable and ensures sustainable agricultural development; the promotion of pilot projects that are appropriate and likely to be adequately maintained; the initiation of rural energy programmes supported by technical training, banking and related infrastructure; and the intensification of research and development, diversification and conservation of energy (paras. 14.93 and 14.95).

Conclusion

47.   Recent decades have witnessed rapid changes in population and socio-economic development, accompanied by increasing environmental stresses at global, regional and local levels. In some cases, deteriorating environmental conditions have had adverse effects on both the populations themselves and the economies that support them. Reversing or even moderating those trends will require efforts on many fronts—those of reassessing national policies, redefining political commitments, and identifying priorities for international cooperation, to name a few. From the conceptual side, careful attention should be given to the examination of two notions in particular which have become very popular when this kind of issue is discussed. The first involves the carrying-capacity of an ecosystem, which is generally understood to refer to the number of people that the ecosystem can support at an acceptable level of quality of life. The second notion involves the identification of possible environmental discontinuities, which are understood to refer to the critical thresholds of irreversible injury to the environment that emerge when ecosystems have been mistreated over long periods of high stress without prominent signs of damage. It is equally important to take into account the following (and thus address some puzzles in terms of future environmental stress): in the not very distant future, the very large numbers of people who are living in what are now called less developed regions will be reaching the consumption and production levels that are typical for industrialized countries. It is nevertheless expected that as a result of simultaneous efforts on all of the above fronts, it will be possible to develop a set of economic, social and demographic policies that both improve the state of the environment and increase the quality of life of the world population. It should be acknowledged that substantial progress has been achieved over the years with respect to the traditional topics of population research and natural resources and energy consumption patterns. What has been slow to develop is the interdisciplinary linkage between this type of research, which would make possible better forecasting and projections of environmental effects, and the manner in which the different factors interact with each other. Furthermore, a better understanding of the connections and mutual interactions among the three elements, as proposed by the World Population Plan of Action, still remains an unresolved issue and one of great concern.

48.   The Programme of Action, adopted at the International Conference on Population and Development, confirms the principles and recommendations of the World Population Plan of Action regarding the need to consider the complex nature of population/development/environment interactions and builds upon and further develops the conceptual approach of Agenda 21. The Conference also recognized that population factors are sometimes powerful inhibitors of sustainable development and recommended several actions to facilitate a better integration of population and environmental concerns into the process of social and economic development. On a more technical level, the Programme of Action recommends that governments:

(*a*)   Integrate demographic factors into environment impact assessments;

(*b*)   Utilize demographic data to promote sustainable resource management, especially of ecologically fragile ecosystems;

(*c*)   Undertake periodic reviews of national and international development strategies with the aim of assessing progress towards integrating population into development and environment programmes.

NOTES

[1]General Assembly resolutions 1710 (XVI) and 1715 (XVI) on the first United Nations Development Decade were adopted on 19 December 1961; resolution 2626 (XXV) on the International Development Strategy for the Second United Nations Development Decade was adopted on 24 October 1970; resolution 35/56 on the Third United Nations Development Decade was adopted on 5 December 1980), and resolution 45/199 on the Fourth Decade was adopted on 21 December 1990.

[2]See General Assembly resolution S-18/3 of 1 May 1990, annex, para. 2.

[3]General Assembly resolution 41/128 of 4 December 1986, annex.

[4]For a full assessment, see FAO/WHO, *Nutrition and Development: A Global Assessment*, (Rome, December 1992).

III. GENDER EQUALITY AND THE EMPOWERMENT OF WOMEN

49.   The equality of women and men is recognized in the Universal Declaration of Human Rights[1] and other important international instruments, including the World Population Plan of Action and the recommendations for its further implementation. More recent international conferences, such as the United Nations Conference on Environment and Development (United Nations, 1993b) and the World Conference on Human Rights (United Nations, 1993e) have reaffirmed the international commitment to gender equality and have urged the adoption of measures to improve the status of women. The Plan of Action (paras. 14 (b), 15 (e) and 41-43) and recommendations 5-10 of the Mexico City recommendations express the urgency of promoting the status of women as an end in itself and emphasize the close relationship between the condition of women and other demographic phenomena. Although no single indicator can capture the multiple dimensions of the condition of women, the discussion of the two following issues—gender equality and education—provides some examples that help to assess the degree of progress made. The sections below on adolescents (paras. 155-159) and maternal mortality (paras. 181-195) also provide relevant information on the condition of women.

Issue No. 4.   Achieving gender equality

50.   It has been widely accepted that the elimination of discrimination against women and the achieving of gender equality are aims grounded in basic human rights, whose realization is also essential to achieving sustainable development. In response to the principle of gender equality reiterated at the 1975 World Conference of the International Women's Year (United Nations, 1976), in the Convention on the Elimination of All Forms of Discrimination against Women, adopted by the General Assembly in its resolution 34/180 of 18 December 1979, at the 1980 World Conference of the United Nations Decade for Women: Equality, Development and Peace (United Nations, 1980) and in the 1985 Nairobi Forward-looking Strategies for the Advancement of Women (United Nations, 1985), the need to achieve the full integration of women in society on an equal basis with men has moved to the forefront of the global agenda, and female education has been identified as a priority area for national action in many countries.

51.   Progress towards achieving gender equality is being reviewed as part of the preparations for the Fourth World Conference on Women, to be held at Beijing in 1995. According to recent data on social indicators aimed at capturing the condition of women worldwide (United Nations, 1990), it can be observed that despite the availability of a large number of internationally approved instruments and the important progress made in imple-

menting them, the improvement of women's situation has been found to be much slower than expected. Although institutional and legal barriers to the emancipation of women have been removed increasingly, change in deep-rooted beliefs and habits that govern gender relationships has been slow. In 1990, the Commission on the Status of Women undertook a five-year review and appraisal of the implementation of the Nairobi Forward-looking Strategies and found that the situation of women had deteriorated in many parts of the world, especially in the developing countries where economic stagnation, rapid population growth, the growing burden of debt and the reduction of public expenditures on social services had constrained the opportunities for enhancing women's situation in the spheres of education, employment and health.

52.   By 1989 the number of Governments that have signed and ratified or acceded to the Convention on the Elimination of All Forms of Discrimination against Women was 94. It is encouraging to observe that by the end of 1993, 130 States had ratified or acceded to the Convention. While considerable progress has been achieved in eliminating *de jure* discrimination, less has been made in eliminating de facto discrimination. The Commission on the Status of Women found that many States are beginning to make use of positive action as a means of reducing the gap between discrimination in law and that in practice (United Nations, 1992a). Among the many areas that are related to gender equality and population variables, those that have been studied most involve women's education and economic participation, which have been found to have powerful relationships with the major demographic variables. The impact of women's education is considered separately below, in the discussion of issue No. 5.

53.   Women's employment and income-earning ability have important effects on their own status and on such demographic and family processes as marriage, level and timing of fertility, and arrangements for care of dependants (see chap. IV below). Even though the economic contribution of women is greatly underestimated in the statistics on labour force participation, currently available data indicate that in all parts of the world women make up substantial proportions of the economically active populations. In 1990, 34 per cent of the labour force worldwide was female. The proportion varies considerably from region to region. In industrialized countries, it was somewhat larger (42 per cent) than in developing countries (33 per cent). In most regions the proportion of women counted as being economically active has been increasing.

54.   Working women tend to be paid less than men, both because women are concentrated in low-wage occupations and because they often receive less for performing the same or similar jobs. However, information about the degree of wage disparity is not often available at the national level. A review of wage levels of women and men for 14 developed countries and 10 developing countries found that in no case did women's wages equal those of men. The closest was Iceland, where women's wages came to 90 per cent of men's wages in 1986, and the disparities tended to be small in the Scandinavian countries as well. At the other extreme, women's earnings were only 52 per cent

of those of men in Japan and 50 per cent in the Republic of Korea (United Nations, 1990a).

55. Most women's household work is not counted as economic activity, and much of women's work outside the formal wage sector is missed in standard statistics dealing with employment. Women's work in agriculture, especially subsistence agriculture, is often undercounted. Recent years have seen considerable attention being given to ways of improving statistical indicators of women's economic activity and, more broadly, gender differences in economic status. At the international level, the Statistical Division of the Department of Economic and Social Information and Policy Analysis of the United Nations Secretariat, the ILO and the International Research and Training Institute for the Advancement of Women (INSTRAW) have been working actively in this area, with attention being given to changes in the way key concepts are defined, problems of achieving adequate measurement in practice, and the publication of economic statistics on a gender-specific basis. However, classifications of economic activity and production that are employed for national economic accounting purposes cannot be expected by themselves to provide adequate information for the range of policies and programmes related to gender, population and development issues. The United Nations Expert Group Meeting on Population and Women, held in preparation for the 1994 International Conference on Population and Development, noted a number of critical data and research needs, including information on women's and men's and children's diverse economic, domestic and resource management roles and use of time to fulfil those roles.

56. Another area receiving increasing attention is the one related to male responsibilities and participation. The 1984 International Conference on Population recommended the active involvement of men in all areas of family responsibility, including family planning, child-rearing and housework, so that family responsibilities could be fully shared by both partners (recommendation 9). There is clear recognition that men should assume major responsibilities in controlling their own sexual behaviour and the consequences of that behaviour and should take part more actively in family planning and other family responsibilities, to ensure safe motherhood, respect for girls' and women's rights, support of gender equality, and the elimination of all forms of violence, including physical violence, of which women are often victims.

57. During the period under consideration, it was widely recognized that achieving gender equality and improving the status of women were ends in themselves, regardless of any demographic goal. At the same time, it has been recognized that improving the status of women has important demographic impacts, particularly on mortality and fertility levels, and that attention to gender issues within population activities needs to be more explicitly articulated and strengthened. It is recognized that women face great difficulties in protecting themselves and their children from sexually transmitted diseases, including human immunodeficiency virus (HIV) and AIDS, and that improving women's status may be vital for combating the spread of those diseases. There is an urgent need for programmes aimed at halting the spread of AIDS and other sexually transmitted diseases to be tailored to

the specific needs for information and services of women and men. The following critical areas of concern and action in the coming years have been identified during the preparatory process for the International Conference on Population and Development (Cairo, 1994) and the Fourth World Conference on Women (Beijing, 1995):

(a) The persistent and growing burden of poverty on women;

(b) Inequality in access to education, health and related services and means of maximizing the use of women's capacities;

(c) Violence against women;

(d) The effects of armed conflict or other kinds of conflict on women;

(e) Inequality between men and women in the sharing of power and decision-making at all levels;

(f) Insufficient mechanisms at all levels to promote the advancement of women;

(g) Lack of awareness of, and commitment to, internationally and nationally recognized women's rights;

(h) Insufficient use of mass media to promote women's positive contributions to society;

(i) Lack of adequate recognition of and support for women's contribution to managing natural resources and safeguarding the environment.

Issue No. 5. Women's education and its demographic impact

58. At the individual level, the education of women has come to be viewed as a key element in the improvement of their status. Yet it also offers benefits at the societal level. For both reasons, the importance of educating women has received major attention, particularly in the context of developmental strategies and population policy. In most of the developing world, the long, historical neglect of women's education has left very high illiteracy rates, especially among older and rural women. According to UNESCO sources, in 1990 there were 346 million illiterate men and 602 million illiterate women (constituting 34 per cent of the adult female population). The numbers are even more striking for some regions: it is estimated that about three quarters of the women aged 25 years or over in sub-Saharan Africa and in Southern and Western Asia cannot read or write. For those women, illiteracy contributes to their marginalization within the family, the workplace and public life.

59. Better prospects are observed among younger generations. The rapid expansion of the national educational systems in the developing countries during the past three decades has led to a significant reduction in illiteracy rates among young women. During the period 1970-1990, for instance, the percentage of illiterate women aged 20-24 fell from 19 to 8 per cent in Latin America, from 38 to 12 per cent in Eastern and Western Asia, and from 80 to 49 per cent in sub-Saharan Africa.

60. The unanimous adoption of universal primary education as a fundamental right and as an explicit developmental objective led to a significant growth in educational investment and to a rapid expansion of school systems

during the 1960s and the 1970s, and this resulted in a dramatic global increase in enrolment rates. Educational gains for girls in the developing world were substantial. The estimated proportion of girls aged 6-11 enrolled in schools in developing countries rose from 38 per cent in 1960 to 66 per cent in 1985. Female enrolment in primary school increased from 24.5 to 60 per cent in Africa, from 43 to 65 per cent in Asia and from 57 to 83 per cent in Latin America and the Caribbean. Important, though more modest, enrolment increases for girls in secondary and higher levels of education were also recorded.

61. Until recently, women have been universally underrepresented at all levels of education. Except for Latin America and the Caribbean, the situation still prevails in most developing countries. Women's enrolment in primary and secondary education lags behind men's by at least 10 percentage points in 66 of 108 countries. The gender gap in educational attainment is greatest in low-income countries and increases at higher levels of training. However, throughout most of the world, a steady trend towards a narrowing of gender disparities in school enrolment is manifest.

62. Rapid population growth in many developing countries is outpacing educational efforts. Although the proportion of youth enrolled in school has experienced a substantial expansion, the absolute number of children not attending school has actually increased. The difficulty of keeping pace with a rapidly growing school-age population usually translates into shortages of school facilities and affects the quality of educational programmes. This trend is expected to continue into the twenty-first century and may further undermine the achievement of educational parity for boys and girls. In this respect, the observed trends that were mentioned above regarding food production and nutrition in sub-Saharan Africa are a matter of major concern.

63. The links between female education and demographic behaviour are extensively reviewed in the literature and increasingly taken into account in policy-making. Numerous studies indicate that education influences decisively a woman's overall health, her access to paid employment and her control over family size and birth-spacing, as well as the education and health of her children. Education empowers women with knowledge that allows informed choice in family and non-family matters, enables them to assume a status and identity beyond those connected with child-bearing, and provides exposure to new values that are likely to enhance autonomy. Those benefits go beyond the individual level in that the broadening of choices for women allows them to contribute more fully to the achievement of societal goals. Accordingly, the need to improve women's education has been advocated repeatedly at both academic and political forums as a means of both promoting development and reducing the levels of fertility in the developing world.

64. Much research has been devoted to exploring the links between women's education and fertility. The World Fertility Survey (WFS) and the more current Demographic and Health Surveys (DHS) programme, which cover a large number of developing countries, have greatly enlarged the empirical basis for documentation of this relationship and for development of new

theoretical perspectives. National and cross-national studies based on the data obtained have shown that the association between education and fertility is far more complex than was assumed in the past, since it is contingent on level of development, social structure and cultural milieu. Those studies have explored the multiplicity of channels through which education affects reproductive behaviour. In particular, they have documented how female education delays entry into marriage, influences the normative orientation towards smaller families, and increases awareness and acceptability of, and access to, fertility regulation.

65. In the poorest and least literate rural societies, small improvements in female education may, in the short run, result in an increase in fertility through improvements in maternal health and reductions in breast-feeding and post-partum abstinence. However, there is sound evidence that changing reproductive norms and contraceptive behaviour through enhanced women's education will lead to fertility reduction in the long run. Even at low levels of development, education has a sizeable negative effect on fertility after a threshold, which is usually identified with the level of completed primary education, is reached. The consistent finding that female education has a larger impact on fertility than does male education gives strong support to the general argument for reducing gender disparities in educational attainment.

66. Most studies have focused on the effect of parental education on fertility, but there is increasing evidence that the schooling of children has an important link with fertility as well. The universalization of mass education modifies not only the perception of children-related costs but also intergenerational attitudes and economic relationships within the family, and this leads to lower fertility. The relationship between education and health is also firmly established in the literature. Education is closely linked to child mortality, disease and nutrition. The evidence is unequivocal: educated parents, particularly educated mothers, have better-nourished children and are better health-care providers; consequently, their children are less likely to die in infancy and childhood. The Demographic and Health Surveys, which provide more detail on children's health than was previously available, confirm this conclusion—namely, that maternal education plays a larger role in determining a child's chances of survival than any other socio-economic factor.

67. Governments are increasingly aware of the links between women's education and demographic goals. According to information from the Population Policy Data Bank, two thirds of Governments consider that the status of women has a significant influence on demographic goals. The same source indicates that 56 per cent of Governments have adopted measures related to improving the status of women with a view to influencing demographic trends as well. The role of international organizations has been important in raising awareness regarding the need to enhance women's conditions of life. At the present time, there is a widely shared realization that the implementation of demographic goals requires the promotion of women's status.

68. However, despite universal recognition that women's education is crucial in the development process and that gender-based inequality of ac-

cess to educational and training resources has critical consequences for women's productive and reproductive roles, as well as for their health status and families, the achievement of universal literacy and educational parity with men is still far from being accomplished. Hence, the implementation of programmes aimed at enhancing women's educational assets needs to be further strengthened.

NOTE

[1] General Assembly resolution 217 (III) A.

IV. THE FAMILY: ITS ROLES, COMPOSITION AND STRUCTURE

69.   The World Population Plan of Action affirms that the family is the basic unit of society and should be protected by appropriate legislation and policy (para. 14 (g)). In all parts of the world, families perform important socio-economic and cultural functions. In spite of the many changes that have altered their roles and functions, families continue to provide the natural framework for the emotional, financial and material support essential to the growth and development of their members, particularly infants and children, and for the care of other dependants, including the elderly, disabled and infirm. The family in all its forms is the cornerstone of the world community. As primary agents of socialization, families remain a vital means of preserving and transmitting cultural values. In a broad sense, families can, and often do, educate, train, motivate and support their individual members, thereby investing in their future growth and acting as a vital resource for development. Families are also important agents of sustainable development at all levels of society and their contribution is decisive for success in this area. The specific functions of families include establishing emotional, economic and social bonds among all family members; providing a framework for procreation and sexual relations between spouses; protecting family members; giving a name and status to family members, especially to children; and providing basic care, socialization and education of children.

Issue No. 6.   Diversity of family structures and composition

70.   Along with the almost universally recognized roles attributed to the family, it is important to acknowledge the numerous forms in which families are organized. Such variety is a concomitant of the multiplicity of the forms of social organization, and cultural and religious values. In this respect, the Plan of Action does not endorse any particular form of family over others. As a social unit, the family has been undergoing radical transformations in its formation and structure over the past two decades, owing to demographic and major socio-economic changes. In the developed countries, with the end of the marriage boom in the post-1960s, the entry into matrimony and hence the formation of families has been considerably delayed. Formalized marriage has been losing its status, especially in Western countries, where cohabitation without marriage has increased, at least before children are born. Those changes have been affecting family formation in general and have led particularly to a decrease in the overall prevalence of marriage among women. The number of divorces has also been rising in most countries. Severe inequalities in the division of labour and in the distribution of power also exist within many families. The discussion on the rights of children to decide on their own affairs has only just begun. Egalitarian

26

possibilities for both genders are but words in most families, and a true partnership between men and women on the basis of equal rights and responsibilities is the challenge of modern families. Many of these changes are now beginning to appear in the developing countries.

71.   In the developing countries exhibiting a rapid process of modernization, the mean age at marriage has risen significantly, owing particularly to a notable increase in female education, and this has implied a delay in the formation of families. Data confirm that in almost all industrialized and developing countries between the 1960s and the 1980s, and even more so between the 1970s and the 1980s, the singulate mean age at marriage of women increased.[1] The magnitude of the increments varies from region to region. In Africa, despite signs of a trend towards postponement, the average age at marriage for women is still quite young and contributes to the maintenance of high-fertility patterns in most countries, especially in sub-Saharan Africa where most countries have a singulate mean age at marriage below 21 years. In Latin America and the Caribbean, by the 1980s the singulate mean age at marriage usually exceeded 20 years, but the effect of marriage postponement as opposed to the effect of contraceptive use on fertility levels is more difficult to ascertain in countries where there is high prevalence of consensual and visiting unions. In Asia, marriages have been delayed to varying degrees in recent years, and by the late 1980s, the singulate mean age at marriage exceeded 21 years among women, except in Southern Asia.

72.   The less developed regions are also characterized by traditionally larger differences between the sexes in the singulate mean age at marriage than the more developed countries. During the 1980s, differences exceeding five or six years were not uncommon in the less developed regions, whereas in most countries of the more developed regions they generally varied from two to three years. Northern America, Europe and the former USSR are characterized by a considerable increase in mean age at first marriage, a significant decline in marriage prevalence and an increase in the proportion of those remaining unmarried. In the Scandinavian countries, the proportions of those ever married were very low. The increase in the proportion remaining unmarried, however, has been largely accompanied by the increase in unmarried cohabitation in those countries. During the period 1974-1994, it could also be observed that Governments made important advances in eliminating forms of coercion and discrimination in relation to marriage.

73.   Family structures and composition area affected by other socioeconomic and political changes. In the 1970s and 1980s, for example, some Asian and African countries experienced large-scale international migration owing to a great shortage of labour in the oil-rich countries and internal political conflict. Recently, there has been large-scale migration from Eastern to Western Europe owing to political changes and conflicts. The effects of these migrations on family formation and structure are yet to be known, but they need to be considered when policies are formulated.

74.   Family formation and structure are also influenced by changes in the value system of societies. In fact, the process of modernization has height-

ened the value of attaining higher education and entering the labour market, while the attraction of a traditional child-bearing career for women has declined. In fact, an increasing number of women are attaining higher education and entering the labour market. These changes in the developed countries have significantly modified the lifestyles of both men and women and have produced new aspirations that entail a smaller number of children. Similar trends are gradually appearing in the developing countries, where rapid industrialization and economic development are taking place.

75.   Significant breakthroughs in contraceptive technology, coupled with increased acceptance and use of contraceptives have made possible the achievement of low fertility levels in the developed countries and the initiation of a process of rapid fertility decline in many developing countries. Such rapid declines in fertility in some Asian and Latin American countries have contributed to declines in the size of households.

76.   In all developed countries except the former USSR, the average household size declined through the 1970s. Given the already small size of households, the absolute changes during the period were small—in many cases, between 0.2 and 0.4 persons, or less. However, the trend was discernible and seemed to be continuing through the 1980s, in countries where data were available. For instance, the North American household continued to shrink in size from 3.1 persons in 1970 to 2.7 in 1980, and further to 2.6 persons in 1990. Reduction in household size is also a trend that characterizes most countries in Eastern and South-eastern Asia and in Latin America. China, which contains more than one fifth of the world population, had a moderate household size of 4.4 persons in 1982 and 4.0 persons in 1990. The decline in household size was particularly evident among countries that experienced a significant decline in fertility. On the other hand, there were countries in Africa and in Southern and Western Asia where increases in average household size were reported. For example, the average household size in Algeria increased from 5.9 persons in 1966 to 7.0 persons in 1987. In Pakistan, the size grew from 5.7 persons in 1968 to 6.7 persons in 1981. All countries in Western Asia, except Israel and Turkey, reported an increase in their already high average household size of six or more; this was largely due to a decline in mortality among children and older age groups between the 1970s and the 1980s.

77.   Household composition varies within and between regions. In the majority of African countries, average household size is almost equally divided between children and adults, with a range of five to six members per household. In most Latin American countries the mean number of adults per household in the 1980s was close to 3.0 and was higher than the number of children. Similarly, the majority of Asian countries had 3.0 or more adult members per household, and the mean number of children per household was always smaller than that of adults. In China, Hong Kong, the Republic of Korea and Singapore, a small but growing percentage of the urban elderly no longer live with their adult children. However, the norm is still the extended family, and in rural areas there has been little change from the traditional family structure. The pattern of household composition observed in the developed countries was significantly different from that in developing

countries. In the 1980s, the mean number of children per household varied in the narrow range of 0.5-0.9, and that of adults per household was in the range of 1.9-2.6; however, most of the countries had households with about 2.0 adult members. The presence of two adult members per household in the developed countries is an indication of the predominance of the nuclear type of family; on the other hand, the presence of more than two or three adult members per household in the developing countries indicates the prevalence of an extended type of family or of a nuclear type of family with adult children present.

78.   In the developed countries, another important demographic change that has contributed to the size reduction of households is the remarkable increase in the number of one-person households. Between the 1970s and the 1980s, the developing countries were experiencing a drastic decline in the proportion of households of five persons or more, possibly suggesting the dissolution of the extended type of household. Also, there had been an increase in the number of one-person households, although the proportions of single-person households in the developing countries, compared to those of the developed countries, remained relatively small. This tendency is more noticeable in those developing countries that are engaged in a rapid process of modernization.

79.   From the policy perspective, one notable change in family formation and structure is the increasing number of households headed by single persons, particularly women. Female headship is common in many parts of the world, and its prevalence is growing in many societies, in both the developed and the developing regions. The proportion of female-headed households among the total number of households ranges from less than 5 per cent in Kuwait and Pakistan to 45 per cent in Botswana and Barbados. A great diversity in the prevalence of female-headed households is observed in each region of the world. Around 1980, both in Latin America and in Africa, the proportion of female-headed households ranged from 10 to over 40 per cent. In Asia, the figures vary within a narrower range at a lower level. No Asian country reports that more than 20 per cent of their households are headed by women. In the developed countries during the 1980s, the range of female-headed households varied from 16 per cent in Spain to 38 per cent in Norway. The chance for formerly married women (widowed, divorced or separated) to become household heads is much higher than for single or married women everywhere in the world. The female headship rates for widowed and divorced/separated women were somewhat higher in the developed countries, where 60-80 per cent of those women were household heads. The corresponding figures for Latin American countries fell in the range of 40-60 per cent. Although the available data refer only to a limited number of African and Asian countries, the headship rates for formerly married women vary greatly. These trends are seen as signs of the vitality and resilience that the family as an institution has shown, despite the many pressures and challenges it has faced. New forms of family life are developing to meet the challenges of the modern world.

Issue No. 7. Socio-economic support to the family

80. To a large extent, perceptions, attitudes and aspirations affecting demographic variables are acquired by individuals through their family life. Families and broader kinship-based support systems, as noted earlier, provide the natural framework for the emotional and material custody essential to the growth and support of their members. Although it is recognized that families should aim at achieving self-sufficiency, in many circumstances families are not and cannot be wholly self-sufficient. The reasons for and the solutions to family problems cannot be found solely in families themselves but rather must include the socio-economic and cultural context in which they exist. This observation highlights the need to develop effective legislation, family policies, services and benefits aimed at strengthening basic family functions, taking into account variations in cultural, social and religious customs, and protecting the basic human rights of family members. Beyond this, there is need to develop "family-sensitive" social and economic strategies, policies and programmes aimed not only at responding to the needs of vulnerable families, but also at identifying the "family impact" of policies and programmes more generally.

81. The Plan of Action and the Mexico City recommendations contain a series of provisions aimed at supporting families in fulfilling their roles in society (para. 39 and recommendation 34, respectively). Families are affected by the dynamics of the societies in which they exist. Over the past few decades, the family has undergone varying degrees of change in structure and functions, some of which have increased their vulnerability and need for socio-economic support, largely depending upon the level of national economic development and diversification. This process has been accelerated by advances in technology and changes in mores and values. In addition to those long-term sustained influences, some short-term influences, such as the migration of workers, natural disasters, war and drastic deterioration in economic conditions, have placed severe pressure on families and family structure in many developing countries. In performing functions vital to the well-being of its members and society, the response of the family to those changes has ranged from adaptation without significant dysfunction to total breakdown. Where the family system has broken down, the pressure on social institutions has generally been extreme. In contrast, where supporting social and economic mechanisms were in place, adaptation occurred, with less disruptive effects.

82. In some developed countries, new laws and social welfare programmes have been instituted to respond to some of the problems that have emerged. Responses to social and economic changes are still evolving in most societies. Since the family is such a fundamental unit of society, a more comprehensive understanding of the consequences of those changes for both individuals and society as a whole must be sought before the appropriate social mechanisms can be put in place. Among the social issues affecting the performance of family functions today is the increasing number of vulnerable families, including single-parent families headed by poor women, destitute families, families that are separated owing to the working conditions of their members, refugee and displaced families, families with members disabled or affected by diseases, and families afflicted with drug abuse, disintegration, do-

mestic violence and child abuse or neglect. Of particular importance is the recognition that single mothers with children form a disproportionate share of the poor. The economic and social insecurities associated with the female-headed household is a matter of great concern, particularly for the development of young children.

83.   There is a continuing need for data collection and analysis directed towards monitoring changes in the structure and dynamics of the family and towards an understanding of the ways in which economic and social trends and policies affect and are affected by changes within families. Some of the important areas needing improved understanding are child-care arrangements and, more broadly, the interactions among women's, men's and children's diverse roles, including their use of time, access to and control over resources, participation in decision-making processes, and changes in their norms, values and beliefs.

84.   Family well-being may depend, to an important degree, on the ability of families to make informed choices concerning fertility. Such choice is a basic right which also has important benefits for maternal and child survival and health. Increased efforts are needed to ensure adequate family-life education which should address such issues as reproduction, sexuality, birth-spacing, and information about sexually transmitted diseases (including AIDS). Equally important are parenting skills which are essential for promoting a deeper understanding of responsibilities in a familial and interpersonal context and family values. Families also play a crucial role in meeting the health requirements of all their members; there is need to support families in this vital role.

NOTE

[1]The singulate mean age at marriage is a good estimate of the average age at marriage obtained from census figures and independent of differences in the age distribution of the population.

31

V.   POPULATION GROWTH AND STRUCTURE

85.   The World Population Plan of Action invited those Governments that considered their current or expected rates of population growth to be hampering their goals of promoting human welfare to consider adopting population policies, within the framework of socio-economic development (para. 17). A similar invitation was made in Mexico City (recommendation 13). For that reason, this chapter first focuses on changes in population growth rates in the past 20 years, and then on the changes in the population structure. The Plan of Action also urged all Governments, "when formulating their development policies and programmes, to take fully into account the implications of changing numbers and proportions of youth, working-age groups and the aged, particularly where such changes are rapid" (para. 63). The Mexico City recommendations made a similar point on the question of policies and also noted the continuing imperative to focus attention on the needs of children and youth in countries where fertility levels were high and on the aged in countries experiencing fertility declines (para. 32).

86.   The following discussion is based on the United Nations *World Population Prospects: The 1994 Revision* (1995a). The revision includes estimates of population size and structure, and levels of fertility, mortality and migration for the world, the more developed and the less developed regions, seven major areas, 22 regions and 223 countries, areas and territories. On the basis of such estimates and other analyses, the United Nations also prepares population projections, which are presented in three variants: high, medium and low. The medium variant indicates the most likely future prospect on the basis of the information and knowledge available for each particular country. All three variants assume, in general, further reductions in current levels of mortality and fertility. Table 1 presents a set of major demographic indicators for seleceted years and periods over 1950-2015 for the world and major areas. These data are based on the above-mentioned medium-variant estimates and projections.

87.   The issue of changing population structure was selected for discussion because it is of critical importance to policy makers as well as to those in the private sector. In fact, there are considerable age variations for many types of economic and social activities and characteristics, including labour force participation, income and needs for a variety of goods and services. People in different age groups are in different stages of the life cycle, so that they have different demands for goods and services. Typical goods and services that are closely related to a particular life-cycle stage include paediatric care, school education, different types of housing, family planning services and obstetric care, nursing homes and other services for the elderly, and geriatric care.

TABLE 1. MAJOR DEMOGRAPHIC INDICATORS, BY MAJOR AREA, 1950-2015[a]

Region and year	Population size (millions)	Annual rate of change (percentage)	Crude birth rate (per thousand population)	Crude death rate (per thousand population)	Total fertility rate	Life expectancy at birth	Infant mortality rate (per thousand births)	Urban population (percentage)	Number of cities with population of 5 million or more[b]
World									
1950......	2 520	1.78	37.4	19.8	4.97	46.4	156	29.3	7
1975......	4 077	1.96	30.9	11.7	4.46	57.9	93	37.7	18
1995......	5 716	1.57	25.0	9.3	3.10	64.4	64	45.2	21
2015......	7 469	1.20	20.0	7.9	2.60	69.9	40	55.5	33
Developed countries									
1950......	809	1.20	22.0	10.2	2.77	66.5	59	54.7	5
1975......	1 044	0.81	16.1	9.4	2.11	71.2	21	69.8	8
1995......	1 167	0.40	12.6	10.1	1.70	74.4	10	74.9	6
2015......	1 224	0.18	11.7	10.7	1.83	77.3	7	81.0	7
Developing countries									
1950......	1 711	2.05	44.5	24.2	6.13	40.9	179	17.3	2
1975......	3 033	2.37	36.2	12.4	5.39	54.6	104	26.7	10
1995......	4 550	1.88	28.3	9.1	3.48	62.3	70	37.6	15
2015......	6 245	1.41	21.7	7.4	2.74	68.5	44	50.5	26
Least developed countries									
1950......	193	1.91	48.1	27.7	6.55	35.7	194	7.1	0
1975......	343	2.47	47.6	21.1	6.68	43.6	147	14.2	0
1995......	575	2.82	42.7	14.9	5.80	51.2	110	22.4	1
2015......	945	2.28	32.4	9.6	4.07	59.4	73	35.9	2
Africa									
1950......	224	2.23	49.2	26.8	6.64	37.8	186	14.7	0
1975......	414	2.66	46.5	19.2	6.55	46.0	131	25.2	1
1995......	728	2.81	41.9	13.7	5.80	53.0	93	34.4	2
2015......	1 204	2.37	32.9	9.3	4.09	60.5	61	47.2	5
Latin America									
1950......	166	2.68	42.1	15.5	5.87	51.4	125	41.6	1
1975......	320	2.44	35.1	9.7	4.98	61.1	80	61.3	4
1995......	482	1.84	26.0	6.9	3.09	68.5	45	74.2	2
2015......	641	1.20	18.8	6.3	2.31	73.2	30	82.1	4

TABLE 1 (continued)

Region and year	Population size (millions)	Annual rate of change (percentage)	Crude birth rate (per thousand population)	Crude death rate (per thousand population)	Total fertility rate	Life expectancy at birth	Infant mortality rate (per thousand births)	Urban population (percentage)	Number of cities with population of 5 million or more[b]
Northern America									
1950......	166	1.80	24.6	9.4	3.47	69.0	29	63.9	0
1975......	239	1.10	15.7	9.0	2.01	71.5	18	73.8	2
1995......	293	1.05	15.8	8.7	2.06	76.1	9	76.3	1
2015......	345	0.78	13.8	8.5	2.10	78.8	6	81.9	2
Asia									
1950......	1 402	1.90	42.8	24.0	5.88	41.3	180	16.8	2
1975......	2 406	2.27	33.9	11.4	5.06	56.3	98	24.6	6
1995......	3 458	1.64	25.2	8.4	3.03	64.5	65	34.6	11
2015......	4 461	1.15	18.8	7.1	2.44	70.8	38	47.8	17
Europe									
1950......	549	0.96	20.9	11.6	2.56	66.1	72	52.2	4
1975......	676	0.60	15.6	10.1	2.14	70.8	25	67.7	5
1995......	727	0.15	11.6	11.2	1.58	72.9	12	73.6	5
2015......	726	0.16	11.0	11.8	1.73	76.1	9	80.1	5
Oceania									
1950......	13	2.21	27.7	12.3	3.84	60.8	69	61.6	0
1975......	21	2.09	23.9	9.6	3.21	66.6	41	71.8	0
1995......	29	1.54	19.2	7.8	2.51	72.8	27	70.3	0
2015......	37	1.18	16.4	7.4	2.35	76.5	17	72.1	0

Sources: World Population Prospects: The 1994 Revision (United Nations Publication, Sales No. E.95.XIII.16); and World Urbanization Prospects: The 1994 Revision (United Nations publication, Sales No. E.95.XIII.12).

[a]Figures shown for the specified years refer to the following time periods: 1950 signifies 1950-1955: 1975 signifies 1970-1975: 1995 signifies 1990-1995: and 2015 signifies 2010-2015, with the exception of population size and urban population, data for which cover the specified years, and number of cities of 5 million or more, data for which cover the years specified in footnote b.

[b]Figures for each region refer to the years 1950, 1970, 1990 and 2010, reading down consecutively.

Issue No. 8. Diversity of rates of population growth

88. As documented in World Population Monitoring, 1993 (United Nations 1995b) Governments' perceptions of their population growth rates have changed considerably over the past two decades, with an increasing number of countries viewing their growth rates as too high (see table 2). In 1993, only 11 per cent of countries perceived their population growth rates as too low (13 per cent of the developed countries and 10 per cent of the developing countries); 45 per cent perceived their rates to be satisfactory (87 per cent of the developed countries, compared with only 28 per cent of the developing countries); and only one of the developed countries (the former Yugoslav Republic of Macedonia) perceived its rates to be too high, compared with 61 per cent of the developing countries.

89. Many Governments have adopted policies aimed at influencing their population growth rate; others follow a policy of no intervention. Since the adoption of the Plan of Action in 1974, an increasing number of countries have decided to adopt policies aimed at lowering their growth rates. Table 3 displays the evolution of the types of interventions followed by Governments during the past two decades. In 1993, 34 per cent of the developed countries had policies aimed at maintaining their current growth rates, compared with only 4 per cent of the developing countries; and only 2 per cent of the developed countries had policies aimed at lowering their growth rates, compared with 53 per cent of the developing countries.

90. The world population grew from 4 billion at the time of the adoption of the World Population Plan of Action in 1974 to 5.7 billion at the time of the International Conference on Population and Development (September 1994). The amount of the increase over 20 years, 1.7 billion, is equivalent to two fifths (more accurately, 42.5 per cent) of the population of the world in 1974. It is interesting to observe that it took the world 123 years to pass from the first billion, around 1804, to the second, in 1927. The next increment of 1 billion took 33 years (3 billion in 1960), and the next billion took 14 years. Only 13 years elapsed before the world population reached 5 billion (1987), and it is estimated that it will take only 11 years more for it to reach 6 billion (1998). Over 90 per cent of the recent population increase will have occurred in the less developed regions of the world.

TABLE 2. GOVERNMENTS' PERCEPTION OF RATES OF POPULATION GROWTH, 1976-1993
(Percentage of countries)

Year	Too low	Satisfactory	Too high	Total
1976......	25.0	47.4	27.6	100.0[a]
1986......	16.5	45.3	38.2	100.0[b]
1993......	11.0	45.3	43.7	100.0[c]

Source: Population Policy Data Bank, maintained by the Population Division of the Department for Economic and Social Information and Policy Analysis of the United Nations Secretariat.
[a]Representing 156 countries.
[b]Representing 170 countries.
[c]Representing 190 countries.

(Percentage of countries)

Year	To raise rate	No intervention	To maintain rate	To lower rate	Total
1976......	19.9	55.1	55.1	25.0	100.0[a]
1986......	15.9	44.7	8.2	31.2	100.0[b]
1993......	11.6	37.4	13.2	37.9	100.0[c]

Source: Population Policy Data Bank maintained by the Population Division of the Department for Economic and Social Information and Policy Analysis of the United Nations Secretariat.

[a]Representing 156 countries.
[b]Representing 170 countries.
[c]Representing 190 countries.

91.   From 1.96 per cent per annum in the period 1970-1975 and a steady 1.73-1.75 per cent per annum in 1975-1990, the world population growth rate is expected to decrease to 1.68 per cent per annum during the quinquennium 1990-1995. Since 1975, the annual growth rate in the less developed regions has decreased slightly, from 2.38 per cent in the period 1970-1975 to 2.01 per cent in the period 1990-1995. The rate in the more developed regions has decreased from 0.86 per cent in the period 1970-1975 to 0.54 per cent in the period 1990-1995. Such declines in the rate of growth are projected assuming a firm continuation of present efforts and policies.

92.   The decline in population growth rates has not yet been translated into a decline in absolute numbers. The annual increment, which was 47 million in the early 1950s, reached 88 million between 1985 and 1990 and is expected to continue to increase to 98 million between 1995 and 2000. Within the less developed regions, the group of the least developed countries has been growing at an even faster pace; its growth rate has increased from 2.47 per cent in the period 1970-1975 to 2.94 per cent in the period 1990-1995. The group is composed of 47 countries and does not represent a large proportion of the world population. It made up 8 per cent of the world population in 1974 and 10.0 per cent in 1992; by the year 2015 it will constitute 13 per cent of the world population (and 14 per cent in 2025). The rate of growth of those countries, which has been increasing until now, is expected to begin to decline at the end of the present quinquennium.

93.   The extremely varied range of national rates of population growth that characterizes the world at present, resulting from various combinations of different levels of fertility and mortality, reflects the position reached by countries in the various stages of transition. One can distinguish four phases of population growth:

(*a*)   An increase in the growth rate to very high levels, due to decreasing mortality coupled with high fertility;

(*b*)   A decline in the growth rate, due to rapidly declining fertility coupled with declining mortality at moderate rates;

(*c*)   A stagnation in the growth rate at the intermediate level, due to moderate crude death rates and crude birth rates declining at about the same pace;

(*d*) A further decrease to low levels of growth, due to low fertility coupled with an increasing crude death rate, resulting from the ageing of populations.

94. Of the 223 countries, areas and territories included in *World Population Prospects: The 1994 Revision*, about half (104), containing more than two thirds of the total world population, had rates of population growth between 1 and 3 per cent per annum in the period 1985-1990. Among the other countries, 53 (representing 11 per cent of the world population) had growth rates of 3 per cent or more per annum; most were in Africa (24 countries) or in Asia (16 countries). At the other extreme, 66 countries, with 21 per cent of the world population, had growth rates below 1.0 per cent per annum; a majority of them were in Europe (32 countries), but there were also 15 in Latin America, 3 in Asia and 2 in Africa.

95. In addition to the observed differences in the rates of population growth between the more developed and the less developed regions, it is important to observe that while there is a certain degree of homogeneity among members of the first group, such is not the case for the latter. A certain degree of homogeneity in growth rates was perceptible in the period 1965-1970 when Africa, Asia and Latin America had growth rates ranging from 2.4 to 2.6 per cent per annum. Then, the rates increased in Asia, and particularly in Central America and later on in Africa, as mortality rates declined, while South America's rate held steady, owing to concomitant fertility change. During the period 1985-1990 the growth rate increased in Africa to 3.0 per cent per annum, whereas in Asia and Latin America the rates declined to 1.9 and 2.0 per cent, respectively.

96. The above variations in population growth rates are even more pronounced for regions within the major areas. The lowest rates are found in Eastern Asia and the Caribbean (1.3 and 1.5 per cent, respectively), whereas the highest rates belong to Eastern and Western Africa (3.2 per cent). As a result of such trends, the distribution of the world population will manifest important transformations. The population of Europe, which already decreased between 1950 and 1990 from a figure representing 22 per cent of the world population to one representing 14 per cent of the world population, is expected to represent no more than 10 per cent of the world population in the year 2015; and a similar path will be followed by Northern America (representing 6.6 per cent of the world population in 1950; 5.3 per cent in 1990; and 4.6 per cent in 2015). While Asia will continue to hold more than half of the world population (56 per cent in 1950 and 60 per cent in 2015), it is the group of African countries that will increase their proportion significantly (from 9 per cent in 1950 to 16 per cent in 2015).

97. Among the most recent United Nations long-range population projections, the medium-fertility extension assumes that fertility will ultimately stabilize at the replacement level around the year 2100. In this case, it is projected that world population will increase by 89 per cent between 1990 and 2050, reaching a size of 10 billion, then expand by 12 per cent during the following 50 years (2050-2100) to a size of 11.2 billion, and by 3 per cent during the next 50 years (2100-2150) to a size of 11.5 billion. The world pop-

ulation may stabilize ultimately at 11.6 billion people shortly after the year 2200. This figure is higher than that calculated a decade ago, which indicated a stabilization at 10.2 billion around the year 2100.

98.   Other long-range projections produce a wide range of projected population sizes. Evidently, what seem to be minute differences in the total fertility rate can produce completely different results. For example, assuming that fertility stabilized at 5 per cent above the replacement level (in other words, at a total fertility rate of 2.17, instead of 2. 1, children per woman), the world population would reach 20.8 billion in the year 2150 and would still be growing. If fertility stabilized at 2.5 (high variant), the size would be 28 billion in the year 2150 and still growing. If, however, fertility could stabilize at the level of 1.96 children per woman, the world population in the year 2150 would be just 5.6 billion and declining. Any fertility level higher or lower than the replacement level implies a continuous growth or decline in population. It is important to take into account that the level of fertility and the speed of attaining stabilization in the future will depend on the level of social and economic development of each country as well as the effectiveness of Governments' policies and programmes.

Issue No. 9.   Changes in the population structure

99.   The age structure of the population varies among countries and changes over time, with various types of economic and social implications. In the 1950s and 1960s, special attention was drawn to the rapid growth of the child population in the developing countries. The growth in the number of children was faster than that of adults who were responsible for raising and supporting them and was thus considered a threat to economic and social development. This problem remains serious in countries that still have high levels of fertility. In recent years, increasing attention has been given to the ageing of populations in many countries. This demographic trend is also considered to have significant economic and social consequences, particularly for pensions, the size of the labour force, medical care, services for the disabled, family structure and residential patterns.

100.   For the purpose of analysing differential trends in age distribution, it is useful to classify countries in terms of the timing of the initiation of significant fertility decline. The pre-initiation pattern of age distribution trends characterized the least developed countries, mostly in Africa, Southern Asia and Western Asia; the late-initiation pattern was followed by the other less developed regions, mostly in Latin America, Eastern Asia and South-eastern Asia; and the early-initiation pattern was followed by the more developed regions, mostly in Northern America, Europe and Oceania. The populations of the pre-initiation countries, where significant fertility decline had not started by 1990, were very young in 1950 and became increasingly younger for the period 1950-1990. The proportion under age 15 increased from 42 to 46 per cent, the proportion of those aged 65 or over decreased from 3.5 to 2.8 per cent, and the median age declined from 19.1 to 17.0 years.

101.   The trend in age distribution of the late-initiation countries changed direction around 1970, when those countries, on the average, started their fer-

tility decline. Their populations, which had become increasingly younger in the 1950s and 1960s, became increasingly older in the 1970s and 1980s. The proportion under age 15 increased from 37 per cent in 1950 to 42 per cent in 1970 and then declined to 33 per cent in 1990. The proportion of those aged 65 or over tells a slightly different story: it remained at about 4 per cent in the 1950s and 1960s, then rose to 4.9 per cent in 1990.

102. Trends in the early-initiation countries, where fertility decline had started before 1950, were marked by an acceleration in the ageing of their populations. The proportion under age 15 in those countries was 28 per cent in 1950, a figure considerably lower than in the pre-initiation and late-initiation countries. It rose slightly to 29 per cent in 1965, reflecting the "baby boom" observed in a number of countries after the Second World War, then declined steeply to 21 per cent in 1990. The proportion aged 65 or over grew rapidly, from 8 per cent in 1950 to 10 per cent in 1970, and further to 12 per cent in 1990. The median age increased from 28 years in 1950 to 34 years in 1990.

103. It is estimated that as of mid-1990, the proportion of the world population under age 15 was 32 per cent, and of those aged 65 years or over, 7 per cent. In other words, about 1 out of 3 persons on the earth was a child, and 1 out of 16 was an older person. The median age was 25 years, indicating that the world population is still relatively young. There are marked geographical differences in the current age distribution, as shown in table 4, reflecting different past levels of and trends in fertility and mortality. The youngest populations are found in Africa, particularly in Eastern Africa and Western Africa. In those two regions, the proportion under age 15 is about 47 per cent, the proportion aged 65 years or over is below 3 per cent, and the size of the child population is 17 times that of the elderly population. Located at the other end of the spectrum are Northern Europe and Western Europe, where the proportion of those aged 65 years or over is about 15 per cent, and the proportion under age 15 is less than 20 per cent. The sizes of the two groups are comparable in the two regions. The population of Eastern Europe is relatively younger than those of the other more developed regions. Falling between the younger populations in Africa and the relatively older populations in Northern America, Europe, Oceania and the former USSR are the populations of Latin America and Asia. In those two major areas, the proportion aged 65 years or over is about 5 per cent and the proportion under age 15 constitutes about one third of the population.

104. The proportion of the world population under age 15 is projected to decrease from 32 per cent in 1990 to 27 per cent in 2015, and the proportion aged 65 or over will increase from 6 per cent in 1990 to 8 per cent in 2015. Considerable geographical differentials in age distribution are projected to remain during the next few decades. In 2015, Africa will have the highest proportion under age 15 (the projected figure is 39 per cent). At the other end of the spectrum, in Europe and Northern America, the proportion will be about 18-19 per cent. Located in between are Oceania, Asia and the Pacific, and Latin America and the Caribbean, for which the proportion of those under age 15 is projected to be 23-26 per cent in 2015. The largest regional variations within

Major area or region	1950	1975	1995	2015
World				
Under 15......	34.5	36.9	31.5	26.9
Aged 65 years or over......	5.1	5.6	6.5	7.8
Developed regions				
Under 15......	27.3	24.2	19.7	17.4
Aged 65 years or over......	7.9	10.8	13.5	16.6
Developing regions				
Under 15......	37.8	41.3	34.6	28.7
Aged 65 years or over......	3.9	3.9	4.7	6.1
Least developed countries				
Under 15......	41.3	44.9	43.7	38.6
Aged 65 years or over......	3.3	3.1	3.0	3.3
Africa				
Under 15......	42.6	44.7	44.0	39.1
Aged 65 years or over......	3.2	3.1	3.2	3.5
Asia				
Under 15......	36.6	39.9	32.1	25.9
Aged 65 years or over......	4.1	4.2	5.3	7.1
Europe				
Under 15......	26.2	23.7	19.2	16.6
Aged 65 years or over......	8.2	11.4	13.8	16.6
Latin America				
Under 15......	40.2	41.2	33.8	26.3
Aged 65 years or over......	3.5	4.2	5.2	7.3
Northern America				
Under 15......	27.2	25.3	21.9	19.8
Aged 65 years or over......	8.1	10.3	12.6	14.4
Oceania				
Under 15......	29.8	31.0	26.0	23.3
Aged 65 years or over......	7.4	7.5	9.5	11.3

Source: World Population Prospects: The 1994 Revision (United Nations publication, Sales No. E.95.XIII.16).

a major area are expected for Asia where the proportion under age 15 in 2015 will range from 19 per cent (Eastern Asia) to 34 per cent (Western Asia).

105. The order is reversed for the projected proportion aged 65 years or over. The highest proportions are expected for Northern America (14 per cent in the year 2015) and in Europe (17 per cent), followed by Oceania (11 per cent). The lowest proportion (3 per cent) is projected for Africa. Again, Latin America and Asia (7 per cent) will fall between Africa and the major areas composed entirely or predominantly of more developed regions.

106. The above trends and perspectives can be better perceived when represented in the form of dependency ratios (the number of children under 15 years and of adults aged 65 or over per 100 adults in the age group 15-64). At the global level, it can be observed that the world passed from a dependency ratio (minors and elderly per 100 adults) of 66 in 1950 to one of 74 in 1975, and it is expected that the dependency ratio will be 62 in the year 1995 and 54 in the year 2015. While dependency ratios are expected to con-

tinue to decrease in the future, owing mainly to the decline in the proportion of those aged less than 15 years, their values will increase by about 7 per cent in the more developed regions, since the number of the elderly in those regions will increase substantially. A similar pattern may be followed by the less developed regions, but not before the middle of the next century.

107. According to the information available in the Population Policy Data Bank for the late 1980s, only 11 per cent of Governments were satisfied with their respective country's age structure; 40 per cent were unsatisfied; and 7 per cent were very unsatisfied (the remaining 42 per cent did not have any official position). Those Governments that appeared to be unsatisfied were particularly concerned about the high proportion of the population that was below age 15. Among the Governments that specifically alluded to their views on the proportion of the population below age 15, only 7 per cent of Governments reported that they were satisfied.

Issue No. 10. Needs of particular groups of the population

Children and youth

108. The World Population Plan of Action has various provisions aimed at protecting the condition of children, such as the elimination of child labour and child abuse (para. 32 (*e*)), the equalization of the legal and social status of children born in and out of wedlock and/or adopted (para. 40 (*a*)), and the establishment of the legal responsibilities of parents towards the care and support of all their children (para. 40 (*b*)). It asks Governments to take fully into account the implications of changing structures of the population in the formulation of their development policies and programmes (para. 63).

109. Deteriorating social and economic conditions of society usually have a devastating impact on children. In many instances such decay is strongly associated with, or is the root cause of, the growing number of street children, children engaged in prostitution, and child labourers. The girl-child is particularly vulnerable to inequalities in some social groups: she may be the victim of neglect and discrimination with regard to health care, nutrition and education, and in her socialization. Effective action from Governments to protect children from abuse, prevent child exploitation, and deter the increased sex and organ trade which affects children has been weak.

110. On the positive side, however, and among important recent achievements, the Convention on the Rights of the Child, adopted by the General Assembly in its resolution 44/25, recognizes that children are individuals with the right to develop physically, mentally and socially to their fullest potential and to express opinions freely. It also places special emphasis on the primary caring and protective responsibility of the family and stresses the responsibility of each State to do all it can to implement the rights contained in the Convention. In addition, the World Summit for Children, by formulating major goals regarding the survival, protection and development of children by the year 2000,[1] has furthered the likelihood that those rights will be translated into action.

111.   The Programme of Action, adopted at Cairo in 1994, states clearly that its objective of promoting the health, well-being and potential of all children, adolescents and youth is in accordance with the commitments made at the Convention on the Rights of the Child and the World Summit for Children. It provides a series of recommendations which focus on the responsibility of the State to protect young girls and young women and on the needs of subgroups of the population that have emerged as particularly worthy of attention, such as children who are subject to various types of exploitation, abuse and neglect, those who are victims of war and disasters, and street children.[2]

112.   The Programme of Action also urges that equal educational opportunities be ensured for boys and girls at every level, and that educational programmes in favour of life-planning skills, healthy lifestyles and the active discouragement of substance abuse be implemented. It further calls for the active involvement of youth in the planning, implementation and evaluation of development activities that have a direct impact on their daily lives. Moreover, it states that such involvement is especially important with respect to information, education and communication activities and services concerning reproductive and sexual health, including the prevention of early pregnancies, sex education and the prevention of HIV/AIDS and other sexually transmitted diseases. It recalls the special emphasis placed on parental responsibility in the Convention on the Rights of the Child and stresses that access to relevant services, along with confidentiality and privacy as to their use, be ensured, with the support and guidance of parents.

113.   Finally, since the adoption of General Assembly resolution 47/85 in December 1992, youth issues have been highlighted during commemoration of recent international years. For example, the International Year of Indigenous Peoples (1993) addressed the rights and needs of indigenous youth; and in connection with the observance of the International Year of the Family (1994), the linkages between family and youth were emphasized at several United Nations interregional and regional preparatory meetings. The role of youth in the promotion and protection of human rights was also discussed at World Conference on Human Rights (1993). Also, youth-related concerns have been reflected in the preparations for two major conferences scheduled for 1995—namely, the World Summit for Social Development and the Fourth World Conference on Women.

Elderly people

114.   In countries that have managed to lower their population growth rate and now have a growing proportion of aged people, new policies are emerging. Of particular importance is the recognition that among the most vulnerable old people are very old women, whose proportion is rapidly increasing. In response, Governments have established a wide variety of mechanisms and measures to achieve a certain degree of "intergenerational equity", mainly through health-care and income-support systems. There is ample evidence that a large majority of the frail elderly have been receiving support from their relatives, particularly their spouses and children. Equally revealing

is the finding that the elderly and their families may accept assistance from the formal care sector only as a last resort. In spite of the significant progress made in increasing awareness of the contribution that the elderly can make to society and in adopting measures to respond to the needs of older persons (United Nations, 1982), little progress has been made in assessing the magnitude of the physical and human resources needed to accommodate the increasing number of very old people or in preparing guidelines on the appropriate balance between social and family support for them.

115. None the less, the General Assembly, in its resolution 45/106, endorsed the action programme on ageing for 1992 and beyond, as outlined in the report of the Secretary-General on that issue (A/45/420), and invited Member States, the United Nations system and non-governmental organizations to consider innovative and effective ways of cooperating on the selection of targets in the field of ageing, and to participate in the action programme. Following an international conference on ageing that it had convened on the occasion of the tenth anniversary of the adoption of the International Plan of Action on Aging, the Assembly adopted the Proclamation on Aging, in its resolution 47/5. It also decided that 1999 should be observed as International Year of Older Persons.

116. The Programme of Action adopted at Cairo in 1994 recommends that all levels of Government in medium- and long-term socio-economic planning should take into account the increasing numbers and proportions of elderly people in the population; that Governments should provide long-term support and services for growing numbers of frail older people; and that Governments should develop social security systems that ensure greater inter-generational and intra-generational equity and solidarity. It also recommends that Governments should seek to enhance the self-reliance of elderly people in order to facilitate their continued participation in society and recognize their valuable contribution, especially as volunteers and caregivers. In addition, the Programme of Action recommends that Governments, in collaboration with non-governmental organizations and the private sector, should strengthen formal and informal support systems and safety nets for elderly people and eliminate all forms of violence and discrimination against elderly people in all countries, paying special attention to the needs of elderly women.[2]

Indigenous people

117. Indigenous people have also been receiving increased attention. In many regions of the world, indigenous communities experience discrimination and are unable to participate in the mainstream process of social and economic development. Many indigenous communities are different, in demographic terms, from the national populations among which they live. Although they have, in some cases, manifested rapid rates of population growth as a consequence of declining mortality (associated with better access to health and welfare services), in other instances they have not been able to receive the benefits of social and material progress and their survival is in danger. In many instances, they have been forced to leave their natural habitat. Activities aimed at increasing awareness about the rights and concerns of indigenous people

have been carried out by UNESCO for some decades, and that awareness was enhanced by the strong support manifested at the United Nations Conference on Environment and Development in 1992 and more recently by the proclamation in General Assembly resolution 47/75 of 1993 as International Year of the World's Indigenous People.

118.   The Programme of Action adopted at Cairo includes a distinct perspective on the particular needs of indigenous people on population and development. It calls for the development of an understanding of and compilation of data on indigenous people and emphasizes the need to protect their culture and resource base.[2]

Persons with disabilities

119.   The number and proportion of people disabled due to health hazards, accidents or violence is another matter of major concern. The situation of disabled people is critical in poor communities, particularly in the developing countries. In general, people with disabilities are more vulnerable to physical abuse and discrimination than any other group. Unfortunately, the pressing issue of effective measures to prevent disability, facilitate rehabilitation and, particularly, fully integrate disabled persons into society remains unresolved; and in many circumstances, when resources for social programmes are scarce, the disabled community is among the first to suffer from budgetary cuts. On the other hand, more recently, certain Governments have adopted legislative measures addressing the situation of the disabled.

120.   The level of awareness has been enhanced by the United Nations Decade of Disabled Persons (1983-1992) and the adoption of the World Programme of Action concerning Disabled Persons.[3] Subsequently, a long-term strategy to implement the World Programme of Action concerning Disabled Persons was developed in 1993. Finally, in 1994, and for the first time in the context of population conferences, the Programme of Action addressed issues and activities pertaining to persons with disabilities.

NOTES

[1]See *First Call for Children* (New York, United Nations Children's Fund, 1990), or A/45/625, annex, for the World Declaration on the Survival, Protection and Development of Children and the Plan of Action for Implementing the World Declaration on the Survival, Protection and Development of Children in the 1990s, adopted at the World Summit for Children, held in New York in September 1990. These instruments recognized that the implementation of the Convention on the Rights of the Child (adopted by the General Assembly in 1989) is essential to improving children's lives. At the end of 1993, 154 countries had ratified the Convention.

[2]A/CONF. 171/13, chap. I, resolution 1, annex, chap. VI.

[3]See General Assembly resolutions 37/52 and 37/53. The Standard Rules on the Equalization of Opportunities for Persons with Disabilities are contained in the annex to General Assembly resolution 48/96.

VI. REPRODUCTIVE RIGHTS, REPRODUCTIVE HEALTH AND FAMILY PLANNING

121. During the past two decades, an increasing number of countries have adopted various measures aimed at modifying their fertility levels—increasing the availability of family planning services being the most common measure. In addition, increasing numbers of couples and individuals are demanding such services. Particularly noteworthy is the new emphasis on reproductive rights and reproductive health. Although the concept of reproductive health has existed for a number of years, it is not specifically referred to in the Population Plan of Action or in the Mexico City recommendations. Recently it acquired an internationally recognized definition, based on the World Health Organization (WHO) definition of general health. The Programme of Action adopted at Cairo defined reproductive health as a "state of complete physical, mental and social well-being and not merely the absence of disease or infirmity, in all matters relating to the reproductive system and to its functions and processes" (United Nations, 1994b). This definition of reproductive health is broad enough to include sexual health and the provision of services concerning breast cancer, other forms of cancer of the reproductive system, sexually transmitted diseases and HIV/AIDS, and the active discouragement of harmful practices such as female genital mutilation.

122. The role played by reproductive rights, which refer to a set of prerogatives and responsibilities on the part of couples and individuals, is a crucial one for the attainment of reproductive health. Access to family planning information and services is an important instrument for the exercise of reproductive rights. In this chapter, three major issues—namely, the diversity of reproduction patterns and policies, the availability of and access to family planning, and adolescent fertility—are examined.

123. The Programme of Action includes recommendations that address issues that have emerged in the area of reproductive rights and reproductive health since the adoption of the World Population Plan of Action. In addition to providing a precise definition of reproductive health care, the Programme of Action also includes goals for all countries: to make reproductive health-care services available to all individuals through the existing primary health-care system and to remove all barriers to access by the year 2015. Governments are also urged to institute a system of monitoring and evaluating reproductive health services to detect, prevent and control abuses by managers and providers; to give non-governmental organizations an active role in monitoring public-sector programmes; to encourage a broader spectrum of non-governmental organizations and political and community leaders to become involved in the promotion of better reproductive and sexual health; to involve the private sector in the provision of reproductive health-care serv-

ices and cost-recovery strategies; to take positive steps, along with non-governmental organizations, to include women at all levels of the health-care system; to give men a major responsibility in the prevention of sexually transmitted diseases and overall reproductive health; to support integral sexual education and services for children and young people with the support and guidance of their parents; to train guidance providers, such as parents and other community members; and to pay particular attention to victims of sexual violence. The Programme of Action specifies measures that Governments might implement to improve the quality of care in sexual and reproductive health programmes.

Issue No. 11. *Diversity of reproduction patterns and policies*

Levels, trends and prospects of fertility

124. Fertility levels, measured by the total fertility rate (the average total number of children that a woman would have by the end of her reproductive life if current conditions remained unchanged), have continued to decline in all of the world regions in recent decades and are expected to continue to do so in the coming years. World fertility fell by 10.5 per cent—from 3.8 to 3.4 births per woman—between the periods 1975-1980 and 1985-1990, and the magnitude of the decline was projected to reach 13.2 per cent by the period 1990-1995. According to the United Nations publication *World Population Prospects: The 1994 Revision*, the total fertility rate varied from 8.5 (Rwanda) to 1.3 (Italy). Virtually all developed countries have fertility rates that are below the population replacement level (2.1 births per woman). The less developed regions have experienced a significant decline in their level of fertility, from 6.2 births per woman in the period 1950-1955 to 3.6 in the period 1990-1995, and the level is projected to be 2.75 in the period 2010-2015, according to the medium-variant projection of the United Nations. The group of least developed countries has experienced the highest fertility levels, with at least six births per woman, on the average, throughout the period. However, in some of the least developed countries, fertility rates have started to decline and the average is projected to be 4.3 in the period 2010-2015.

125. In the less developed regions, the decline in total fertility rates reached 15 per cent during the periods 1975-1980 and 1985-1990 and is expected to exceed 21 per cent by the period 1990-1995. There are, however, differences within the less developed regions themselves. In most of the regions of Africa, fertility rates remained high, often above six births per woman, and the fertility decline was very small. In the Asian and Latin American regions, fertility tended to converge from rates exceeding 4-5 births per woman towards more moderate levels of 2-4 births per woman, and fertility levels are projected to continue to proceed in this direction. Thus, by the period 1985-1990 the range of average fertility rates had widened in the less developed regions: it was as low as 3.4 in Latin America and 3.5 in Asia, and as high as 6.3 in Africa. It is important to indicate that the observed reductions in the number of births per woman did not produce a comparative decline in the average number of births; in fact, the annual number of births continued to in-

crease. As detailed in *World Population Prospects: The 1994 Revision*, during the past 15 years, in Africa, for example, fertility rates declined by 9.1 per cent, while the number of births increased by 44.1 per cent. At the world level, while rates declined by 13.2 per cent, the number of births increased by 19 per cent during the same period.

126. This situation reflects both the past and the current social, political and economic conditions of those regions. Such conditions affect both economic and social development as well as the degree of success of policies to reduce fertility. Indeed, in general it is in the least developed countries, where the level of development and family planning programme efforts is lowest, that steady high fertility rates are observed. Conversely, in the more modernized countries of Asia and Latin America, where development is progressing and fertility regulation methods are more readily available, fertility has been declining steadily, and sometimes sharply, as is the case in Eastern Asia, for instance, where fertility fell from 2.8 to 2.3 births per woman between the periods 1975-1980 and 1985-1990. In Japan, Singapore, the Republic of Korea and Hong Kong, the total fertility rate fell below the replacement level; and by the late 1980s the total fertility rate had reached levels as low as 1.3 births per woman in Hong Kong.

127. In the more developed regions, where fertility rates below the replacement level were reached as early as the 1970s in a number of countries, fertility has also continued its downward trend. By the period 1985-1990, fertility rates were below 2 births per woman in most developed regions. By 1990, only a few countries—Albania, Ireland, Sweden and the former USSR—had fertility rates exceeding 2.1. On the other hand, exceptionally low rates—as low as 1.3 births per woman—were recorded in Italy and Spain as early as 1989. In recent years, however, a turning-point seems to have been reached in some countries where a slight upward fertility trend has been observed. This is the case notably in the United States of America, several countries of Northern and Western Europe, and New Zealand (United Nations, 1992b).

128. The significance of those fertility patterns differs substantially, however, for the more developed and the less developed regions when changes in fertility are examined in terms of changes in average annual number of births. Indeed, in the less developed regions, between the periods 1975-1980 and 1985-1990, the annual average number of births continued to increase, sometimes considerably, mainly as a consequence of the population momentum resulting from an increase in the number of women of reproductive age, which itself resulted from the high fertility of the past. This increase in the number of births, together with the effects of declining mortality, continues to fuel the increments in population size, despite the decline in fertility rates. Conversely, in Europe, where the overall total fertility rates declined over the past two decades, the average annual number of births also fell. Thus, despite the overall fertility reductions in the world, many countries in the less developed regions still continue to be concerned about increasing population size, whereas countries in the more developed regions have been facing other concerns related to fertility decline, a notably larger ageing population, a shrinking of the labour force and immigration issues.

47

Age patterns of fertility

129.   Besides the differences in their levels of fertility, world regions also show differences in their age patterns of fertility. Those age patterns are influenced by the timing of family formation and the mean age at first marriage, as discussed above (paras. 71 and 72). Assumptions for age-specific fertility rates for the period 1990-1995 show that the less developed regions experience their highest fertility (205 births per 1,000 women) in the age group 20-24, whereas in the more developed regions the highest age-specific fertility rate (only 126 births per 1,000 women) is found in the age group 25-29. When the less developed regions are compared, Africa appears to have the highest age-specific fertility, with an average broad peak pattern of about 275 births per 1,000 women for women aged 20-24 years in the period 1990-1995. Subregional differences reveal, however, that fertility in Northern and Southern Africa is highest at ages 25-29, whereas in the other African subregions the peak value occurs at ages 20-24.

130.   A broad peak also prevails in Asia and Latin America, even though, with an average rate of about 192 births per 1,000 women in Asia and 173 births per 1,000 women in Latin America at ages 20-24, the peak maximum is much lower than in Africa. In Latin America, however, it is expected that completed fertility will be achieved at a younger age than in Asia. Indeed, in Latin America, it is expected that about two thirds of total fertility will be achieved by age 30, as opposed to less than 60 per cent for the Asian subregions, except Eastern Asia where 80 per cent of total fertility occurs by age 30 (figures derived from the values presented in table 5).

131.   In Europe and Northern America, peak fertility occurs at ages 25-29; in this age group, the fertility rate is 117 births per 1,000 women in Europe and 124 births per 1,000 women in Northern America. Overall levels are considerably lower than in the less developed regions, and completed fertility is achieved even earlier: it is expected that about 70 per cent of total fertility will be completed before age 30. In Australia and New Zealand, the fertility tempo is only slightly slower, with 66 per cent of overall fertility achieved before age 30. The former USSR and Eastern Europe deviate significantly from the overall fertility pattern just described: peak fertility is expected to occur in age group 20-24, and in the former USSR reproduction ceases early, with almost 80 per cent of total fertility completed by age 30 (figures derived from table 5).

Policies aimed at affecting fertility levels

132.   It is important to take into account that, although fertility levels are conditioned by complex social and economic structures, the impact of these structural determinants is mediated by three major intermediate sets of variables:

(*a*)   Factors affecting exposure to intercourse (for example, age at entry into sexual unions and abstinence);

(*b*)   Factors affecting conception (for example, levels of fecundity/ infecundity and contraception);

TABLE 5. BIRTHS AND AGE-SPECIFIC FERTILITY RATES FOR MAJOR AREAS AND REGIONS OF THE WORLD, 1990-1995

Major area or region	Total births (thousands)	Total fertility rate (per woman)	Age-specific fertility rate (per 1,000 women)							Percentage of births to women	
			15-19	20-24	25-29	30-34	35-39	40-44	45-49	Under age 20	Age 35 or older
World	**687 422**	**3.1**	**60**	**181**	**177**	**112**	**59**	**24**	**8**	**11**	**11**
More developed countries	72 484	1.7	32	96	111	71	26	5	0	9	9
Less developed countries	614 938	3.5	65	200	194	124	71	31	11	11	11
Least developed countries	114 735	5.8	140	275	273	218	149	79	27	17	14
Africa	**142 412**	**5.8**	**136**	**267**	**272**	**219**	**149**	**82**	**35**	**17**	**15**
Eastern Africa	48 686	6.5	151	305	299	242	166	97	34	17	14
Middle Africa	17 611	6.5	207	305	271	230	163	89	26	23	13
Northern Africa	23 732	4.2	60	187	236	179	112	50	14	10	15
Southern Africa	7 154	4.2	75	198	217	165	98	63	28	12	16
Western Africa	45 228	6.5	164	290	289	240	171	99	56	18	16
Asia	**417 929**	**3.0**	**45**	**186**	**183**	**108**	**56**	**22**	**7**	**8**	**10**
Eastern Asia	123 218	1.9	14	160	134	55	15	4	1	4	4
South-central Asia	206 320	4.1	73	223	237	152	89	38	12	9	14
South-eastern Asia	63 091	3.3	47	162	181	139	87	33	9	11	12
Western Asia	25 299	4.4	65	206	240	173	121	58	21	10	15
Europe	**42 056**	**1.6**	**27**	**98**	**102**	**62**	**23**	**5**	**0**	**8**	**9**
Eastern Europe	17 818	1.6	38	132	89	44	18	4	0	12	7
Northern Europe	6 252	1.8	27	92	125	87	32	6	0	6	10
Southern Europe	7 762	1.4	17	73	99	64	25	6	0	6	10
Western Europe	10 224	1.5	11	66	113	79	29	5	0	3	11
Latin America and the Caribbean	**59 806**	**3.1**	**79**	**173**	**156**	**111**	**66**	**28**	**5**	**15**	**11**
Caribbean	4 069	2.8	78	153	138	95	57	24	8	15	11
Central America	17 762	3.5	89	194	181	126	75	31	8	17	10
South America	37 975	3.0	75	167	149	108	65	27	4	15	12
Northern America	**22 578**	**2.1**	**60**	**113**	**120**	**81**	**32**	**5**	**0**	**13**	**10**
Oceania	**2 642**	**2.5**	**28**	**111**	**163**	**119**	**53**	**20**	**8**	**6**	**14**
Australia-New Zealand	1 594	1.9	24	83	141	98	33	5	0	6	10

Source: World Population Prospects: The 1994 Revision (United Nations publication, Sales No. E.95.XIII.16).

(c)   Factors affecting gestation and parturition (for example, foetal mortality, abortion).

Governments wishing to modify the fertility levels of their country may design policies aimed at modifying the social and economic determinants of fertility and/or the most immediate factors affecting it. The World Population Plan of Action recognizes, as one of its principles, the basic right of couples and individuals to decide freely and responsibly the number and spacing of their children (para. 14 (f)). It also acknowledges the variety of national goals with regard to fertility (para. 27), recommends criteria to be followed in the formulation and implementation of fertility policies (para. 29) and recognizes a series of instruments available to affect fertility (paras. 30-32). Mexico City recommendations 25, 27-33 and 35 not only reaffirmed the provisions of the Plan of Action but also adopted other, complementary, proposals, asking Governments to make family planning universally available, provide education and suitable family planning information to adolescents, improve the quality of services, provide the necessary resources for those programmes, and adopt fertility goals and policies ensuring that programmes were neither coercive nor discriminatory.

133.   Governments' views and policies on fertility levels have changed since the adoption of the Plan of Action. The number of countries perceiving their fertility levels to be too high has been increasing (see table 6). In 1993, 45 per cent of all countries viewed their level of fertility as too high. That number represented 67 per cent of the world population. The gradual shift towards viewing fertility as excessive is the continuation of a long-term trend that was already under way during the period 1976-1986, when the percentage increased slightly from 35 to 40 per cent. The percentage of countries that viewed fertility as too low dipped from 14 per cent in 1986 to 12 per cent in 1993, while those viewing fertility as satisfactory declined from 50 to 44 per cent between 1986 and 1993.

134.   Regarding the policies undertaken to influence the level of fertility (see table 7), the trends closely parallel those in the perceptions of fertility already noted. The percentage of countries intervening to lower fertility increased from 26 to 41 between 1976 and 1993, while the percentage of countries with policies to raise fertility increased slightly during the same period, from 9 to 12. Those countries with a policy of non-intervention declined sharply, from 51 to 33 per cent. Such a global analysis, however, masks much of the diversity that is apparent at a lower level of aggregation. For example, as of 1993, while 63 per cent of the developing countries viewed their fertility level as too high, only one country in a more developed region (Turkey) held this perception. Slightly more than two thirds of developed countries (71 per cent) viewed their fertility level as satisfactory. Those developing countries (5 per cent) that viewed their fertility level as too low were for the most part countries with relatively small populations and low population densities (they have about 1 per cent of the population of the less developed regions). In 1993, 45 per cent of the developed countries adopted a policy of no intervention, and 29 per cent wished to maintain their current fertility levels, whereas 28 per cent of the developing countries adopted a policy of no intervention and only 8 per cent wished to

TABLE 6. GOVERNMENTS' VIEWS ON FERTILITY LEVELS, 1976-1993
(Percentage of countries)

Year	Too low	Satisfactory	Too high	Total
1976......	11.5	53.2	35.3	100.0[a]
1986......	14.1	50.0	40.0	100.0[b]
1993......	11.6	43.7	44.7	100.0[c]

Source: Population Policy Data Bank maintained by the Population Division of the Department for Economic and Social Information and Policy Analysis of the United Nations Secretariat.
[a]Representing 156 countries.
[b]Representing 170 countries.
[c]Representing 190 countries.

TABLE 7. AIM OF GOVERNMENTS' POLICIES TO INFLUENCE FERTILITY LEVELS, 1976-1993
(Percentage of countries)

Year	To raise	To maintain	To lower	No intervention	Total
1976......	9.0	14.1	25.6	51.3	100.0[a]
1986......	11.8	11.2	32.4	44.6	100.0[b]
1993......	12.1	13.7	41.1	33.2	100.0[c]

Source: Population Policy Data Bank maintained by the Population Division of the Department for Economic and Social Information and Policy Analysis of the United Nations Secretariat.
[a]Representing 156 countries.
[b]Representing 170 countries.
[c]Representing 190 countries.

maintain their current levels. For the same year, 12 per cent of Governments had adopted policies aimed at increasing their fertility levels (25 per cent of the developed countries and only 5 per cent of the developing countries); and while only one developed country had adopted a policy to lower its fertility level, 57 per cent of the developing countries had done so. On a more general level, it may be observed that the social justice to be achieved, *inter alia*, through a more equitable distribution of income, land, social services and amenities, as proposed by the Plan of Action (para. 32 (*c*)), is a goal that has not been achieved by many Governments, partially owing to the severe global economic stagnation and recession in many countries over the past two decades.

135.   Going beyond the thrust of past recommendations, which sought to ensure that family planning programmes were not coercive, the Programme of Action encourages Governments to focus most of their efforts on meeting their population and development objectives through education and voluntary measures rather than schemes involving incentives and disincentives. It also urges the international community to establish an efficient coordination system and facilities for the procurement of contraceptive and other commodities essential for sexual and reproductive health programmes in developing countries and countries with economies in transition, and to provide overall support in the area of reproductive and sexual health to the latter without cutting back on the support provided to the former.

136.   There is also increased concern about the effect on human reproduction of new biotechnologies that make possible artificial insemina-

tion, in vitro fertilization, embryo transfers, surrogate motherhood, cryogenic storage of sperm and ova, genetic selection, and prenatal diagnosis, including sex determination. Some of these technological achievements raise such important questions in the field of reproductive rights and reproductive health as: Should embryo studies leading to eugenic practices be permitted? Under which circumstances could these new biotechnologies be used for demographic purposes? Should women beyond a certain age be permitted to have access to medically assisted reproduction, and receive embryo transfers, for example, or be artificially inseminated? Although most of these technologies have as yet no significant demographic impact, of particular concern are issues such as ethical values, human rights violations, and the potential for future alteration of some demographic characteristics, especially the sex composition of populations (United Nations, 1991). The international community should begin to address the above issues and discuss the possibility of adopting a set of international standards, perhaps in the form of a protocol, on use of and access to the new biotechnologies.

137.   Observation of sex ratios at birth (the number of male births per 100 female births) in some countries and some provinces shows a disproportionate number of boys, above the normal range of values. A strong preference for boys in some traditionally patriarchal societies, combined with access to prenatal diagnostic techniques and abortion, is a plausible explanation for those irregularities in sex ratios. It is precisely a concern for this practice that has prompted at least one state government in India to adopt legislation that attempts to control the abuse of prenatal diagnostic procedures that would encourage the use of abortion for gender-selective purposes.

Abortion

138.   Mexico City recommendation 18(*e*) includes a passage that urges Governments to take appropriate steps to help women avoid abortion, which in no case should be promoted as a method of family planning, and whenever possible, to provide for the humane treatment and counselling of women who have had recourse to abortion. This recommendation, the subject of a heated debate at the Conference in 1984, was one of the few instances in which a governmental delegation requested that a separate statement regarding its position on a particular matter be included. The statement indicated that, while joining the consensus, the delegation wanted to affirm that one step towards the elimination of illegal abortion, which represented a very serious health hazard, was the provision of access to abortions that were legal and safe.

139.   One of the major limitations in understanding the nature and the extent of the demand for abortion is the limited availability of reliable statistics. The most common sources refer to official statistics provided by Governments, surveys and hospital admissions.[1] It has been estimated by WHO that approximately half a million women die every year for reasons associated with their reproductive life, and that about 30 per cent of those deaths are due to unsafe abortion. Yet, these figures seem conservative compared to the estimates given in the draft platform for action of the Fourth World Con-

ference on Women, which indicate that every year more than 20 million women terminate unwanted pregnancies through unsafe abortions. This is a result of lack of access to relevant care and services such as family planning, costly contraceptive methods, lack of information and restrictive legislative practices. The figures also indicate that of the 20 million women, 15 million survive but with a wide range of long-term disabilities (United Nations, 1995). The incidence of abortion varies widely between the countries for which abortion data are available. In 1987, in China and India for instance, the number of abortions per 100 live births was estimated to be about 45 and 2, respectively. In the Eastern European countries the corresponding figure sometimes exceeded 100, although it rarely exceeds 30 in the other European regions. It has been estimated that in 1987, between 26 million and 31 million legal abortions and between 10 million and 22 million clandestine abortions were performed world-wide. Action towards a greater liberalization of abortion has been growing recently in many countries, notably in Belgium, Romania and Spain, where access to legal abortion has been made easier by recent legislation, although abortion is far from being available on request. In other European countries, however, notably in Ireland, such efforts have been less successful, and in Poland recent legislation restricted access to abortion to cases where it would be necessary for health reasons.

140. Information available in the Population Policy Data Bank indicates that in 1993, for the 190 countries for which there was such information, 173 countries granted access to abortion when the purpose was to save the life of the mother and 41 made abortion available on request (table 8). No Government appears to have ever sanctioned the use of compulsory abortion to comply with demographic targets.

141. Abortion has been one of the most dividing issues of the past decade. The data presented in table 8 illustrate the access to abortion in different circumstances. It is granted in a more liberal way if the purpose is to save the life of the woman, while it is more restricted, particularly within the group of developing countries, if it is requested for other reasons. Numerous debates nourished by emotional positions and aggravated by a lack of solid data and analyses have not been conducive to better understanding of the complexity of the issue and, consequently, to the adoption of sound courses of action. Nevertheless, there are some elements of consensus that seem to be emerging and that were present in the long discussions held during the preparatory activities of the International Conference on Population and Development and in the Conference itself. Such consensus seems to contain the following elements:

(a) Abortion is resorted to because of lack of sexual education and access to family planning methods, method failure, or other deficiency;

(b) The incidence of abortion should be reduced and the best way to do so is through good prevention;

(c) Enhancement of actions aimed at achieving responsible parenthood, accompanied by improved sexual education, and access to safe and reliable family planning methods are the best means of preventing abortions.

TABLE 8. GROUNDS FOR PERMITTING ABORTION, 1993

Access granted	Number of countries	Percentage of world population	Percentage of countries		
			Total	Developed	Developing
To save the life of the woman...........	173	96	91	93	91
To protect physical health..................	119	75	63	89	52
To protect mental health....................	95	69	50	88	35
In case of rape or incest....................	81	72	43	81	26
In case of foetal impairment..............	78	64	41	84	23
For economic or social reasons	55	44	29	77	9
On request..	41	38	22	59	6

Sources: Abortion Policies: A Global Review, vol. I, *Afghanistan to France* (United Nations publication, Sales No. E.92.XIII.8); vol. II, *Gabon to Norway* (United Nations publication, Sales No. E.94.XIII.2); and vol. III, *Oman to Zimbabwe* (United Nations publication, Sales No. E.95.XIII.24).

Issue No. 12.   Availability of and access to family planning

142.   Family planning services have expanded around the world. The expansion results from the recognition of the right of couples and individuals to decide the number and spacing of their children, as a means of achieving demographic goals or as a health measure, considering that early, late, numerous and frequent pregnancies are all detrimental to maternal and child health. Recent data indicate the following major shifts in the way family planning programmes are conceived and organized:

(*a*)   Emphasis is increasingly being placed on the needs of users, not just on aggregate acceptor figures, and on human rights and health benefits, not just on the demographic impact of programmes;

(*b*)   There is increasing criticism of traditional target systems for family planning workers and more emphasis on integrating such services into health programmes;

(*c*)   There is extensive recognition of the fact that incentive and disincentive schemes to lower or raise fertility have only marginal impact on fertility levels and in some cases are counter-productive;

(*d*)   There is wider acceptance of family planning programmes as constituting good vehicles for confronting the spread of HIV and other sexually transmitted diseases.

Contraceptive use

143.   According to data available through 1993 (see table 9), in 1990 approximately 57 per cent of couples in the world with the wife in her reproductive years were currently using contraception—about 72 per cent in the developed countries and 53 per cent in the developing countries. Considering the lag between the time of data collection and the current period, the level of contraceptive use in the developing countries is likely to have been about 55 per cent in 1993. Regional differences in levels of use remain large.

144.   Methods used by women make up about two thirds of contraceptive practice worldwide, and such methods have been increasing their share

TABLE 9.   AVERAGE PREVALENCE OF SPECIFIC CONTRACEPTIVE METHODS, BY REGION, 1990

| Region | All methods (1) | Modern methods^a (2) | Sterilization | | Pill (5) | Inject-able (6) | Intra-uterine device (IUD) (7) | Condom (8) | Vaginal barrier methods (9) | Rhythm (10) | With-drawal (11) | Other methods (12) |
			Female (3)	Male (4)								
Percentage of couples with the woman in the reproductive ages												
World	57	49	17	5	8	1	12	5	1	3	4	1
Less developed regions	53	48	20	5	6	1	13	2	0.3	2	2	1
Africa	18	14	2	0.1	7	2	3	1	0.2	2	1	1
Northern Africa	40	35	2	b	19	0.2	12	2	0.3	2	2	0.4
Sub-Saharan Africa	13	9	1	0.1	3	2	1	0.5	0.1	2	1	1
Asia and Oceania^c	58	54	23	7	4	1	16	3	0.2	2	2	1
Eastern Asia^c	79	79	33	10	3	0.2	31	2	0.2	1	0.1	0.2
Other countries	42	36	15	4	5	2	5	4	0.2	2	3	1
Latin America and the Caribbean	58	48	21	1	16	1	6	2	1	5	3	1
More developed regions^d	72	50	8	4	16	0.1	6	14	2	8	13	2
Percentage of contraceptive users												
World	100	85	30	9	14	2	21	9	1	6	7	2
Less developed regions	100	91	38	10	11	3	25	5	0.5	4	3	2
Africa	100	78	8	0.4	37	10	18	4	1	10	6	5
Northern Africa	100	89	6	b	48	0.4	30	4	1	5	5	1
Sub-Saharan Africa	100	70	11	1	28	18	8	4	1	15	7	9
Asia and Oceania^c	100	93	39	11	7	2	28	5	0.4	3	3	2
Eastern Asia^c	100	99	41	12	4	0.2	39	2	0.3	1	0.1	0.3
Other countries	100	84	37	10	11	5	11	8	1	6	6	3
Latin America and the Caribbean	100	83	36	1	28	2	11	4	1	9	6	2
More developed regions^d	100	69	11	6	22	0.2	8	20	3	11	18	2

Source: World Contraceptive-use Data Diskettes, 1991: User's Manual (United Nations publication, ST/ESA/SER.R/120); and data files maintained by the Population Division of the Department for Economic and Social Information and Policy Analysis of the United Nations Secretariat.

NOTE: These estimates are based on recent available survey data (average date, 1990) and reflect assumptions about contraceptive use in countries with no data.

^a Including methods in columns 3-12.
^b Data unavailable.
^c Excluding Japan.
^d Australia, New Zealand, Europe, Northern America and Japan.

in total contraceptive use. The most widely used methods are female sterilization, accounting for 30 per cent of contraceptive use worldwide, intrauterine devices (IUDs) (21 per cent) and oral pills (14 per cent). The main methods used by men—condoms and vasectomy—each account for 9 per cent of contraceptive use, while "couple" methods—chiefly natural family planning (rhythm) and withdrawal (coitus interruptus)—account for about 13 per cent of contraceptive use. Although there remain many countries in Africa and several in other regions where the level of contraceptive use is still very low, most developing countries that have available data on trends have experienced a substantial increase in the level of contraceptive use. Even in sub-Saharan Africa, recent surveys show an increase in levels of use in Botswana, Cameroon, Kenya, Lesotho, Namibia, Rwanda, Swaziland, South Africa and Zimbabwe.

145. As shown in table 9, there are some striking differences in the contraceptive method profiles for the different regions of the world. For example, the percentage of female sterilization in Latin America and the Caribbean, Asia and the Pacific, and Oceania is about 3.5 higher than in the more developed regions or in Africa. The selection of this method is even more striking when compared to that of male sterilization in those regions, which is similar to the percentage of female sterilization in other regions. In turn, at 39 per cent, IUD appears to be a close second preferred method of choice for East Asia (which has the highest percentage of use for this method) and four times the percentage of IUD use for the more developed regions. As for women using the pill, the percentage in Northern Africa is more than four times that in the other less developed regions and more than double that in the more developed regions. As for injectable methods, whereas the worldwide use is 2 per cent, in sub-Saharan Africa it is 18 per cent, in contrast to 0.2 per cent in the more developed regions and 2 per cent in Latin America and the Caribbean, Asia and the Pacific, and Oceania. Interestingly, sub-Saharan Africa has a similar percentage of those selecting injectables and those practising the rhythm method, with the percentage of those practising the latter (15 per cent) at close to four times the percentage (4 per cent) of those in the less developed regions as a whole. The percentage of those practising withdrawal in the more developed regions (18 per cent) is six times that of those in the less developed regions (3 per cent). Finally, the percentage of condom use in the more developed regions (20 per cent) is four times the percentage of its use in the less developed regions (5 per cent)—with added implications in terms of the use of condoms for the prevention of sexually transmitted diseases.

Availability of contraceptives

146. The World Population Plan of Action considers that the recognition of the above-mentioned right of couples and individuals also implies the provision by Governments of the means to achieve the desired number and spacing of children (see Mexico City recommendations 25, 27 and 28). Governmental policies on access to modern contraceptive methods changed during the period 1974-1993. The major change was reflected in the fact that an increasing proportion of Governments provide direct support (services are

provided by a governmental agency) rather than indirect support (the Government funds a non-governmental organization which then provides the services). The proportion of countries where governmental policy limited access to contraceptive methods declined from 7.1 per cent in 1974 to 3.5 per cent in 1986 and to less than 2 per cent in 1993. For example, in 1974, direct support was provided by 55.1 per cent of Governments; the proportion increased to 71.8 per cent in 1986 and to 81.6 per cent in 1993 (table 10). A greater proportion of the developing countries (86.4 per cent), compared with the developed countries (73.2 per cent), provided direct support for contraceptives in 1993. In 1974, 70.5 per cent of Governments offered direct or indirect support for modern methods of contraception; in 1986, 85.9 per cent of Governments provided direct or indirect support; and, according to *World Population Monitoring, 1993* (United Nations, 1995b), by 1993, this proportion had reached 89 per cent (85.7 per cent of the developed countries and 90.3 per cent of the developing countries).

147.   In the 1980s there was rapid progress in extending the availability of contraception in the developing countries.[1] Asia and the Pacific (except Western Asia) and Latin America and the Caribbean are the developing regions where contraceptives are most widely available. Availability continues to be most limited in sub-Saharan Africa (where it is estimated that under 40 per cent of the population has ready access to any method), followed by Northern Africa and Western Asia. The countries in transition from centrally planned to market economies manifest a high over-reliance on abortion for fertility regulation purposes, and women in those countries clearly need access to contraception on an urgent basis. However, all regions have experienced an impressive increase in contraceptive availability in the past two decades, particularly, between 1982 and 1989, as shown in table 11.

148.   Although availability of all the major contraceptive methods increased during the 1980s, there is still no wide choice of methods in most developing countries. A survey reported in *World Population Monitoring, 1993* (United Nations, 1995b), covering 97 developing countries estimated the percentage of each country's population that had ready and easy access to specific contraceptive methods in 1989. Widespread availability of at least one method—defined as ready access for four fifths or more of the national population—was estimated to exist in 28 per cent of the countries. However, in only 8 per cent was there widespread availability of four or more methods. Using a lower standard, the survey showed ready availability for half or more of the national population, ready access to at least one method in 50 per cent of the countries, and availability of four or more methods for only one quarter of the countries.

149.   Contraceptive availability does, however, tend to be above the average in most of the largest countries, including Bangladesh, Brazil, China, India, Indonesia and Mexico. The most widely available methods are condoms and oral contraceptives ("the pill"), estimated to have been readily available to roughly 70 per cent of the population of the developing countries in 1989 (table 11). Female sterilization is judged to have been readily available

TABLE 10. GOVERNMENTS' POLICIES CONCERNING ACCESS TO
CONTRACEPTIVE METHODS, 1974-1993
(Percentage of countries)

Year	Access limited	Access not limited			Total
		No support	Indirect support	Direct support	
1974......	7.1	22.4	15.4	55.1	100.0[a]
1986......	3.5	10.6	14.1	71.8	100.0[b]
1993......	1.6	9.5	7.4	81.6	100.0[c]

Source: Population Policy Data Bank maintained by the Population Division of the Department for Economic and Social Information and Policy Analysis of the United Nations Secretariat.

[a]Representing 156 countries.
[b]Representing 170 countries.
[c]Representing 190 countries.

to 65 per cent of the population, IUDs to 62 per cent and male sterilization to 57 per cent, in 1989.

150. Providing access to modern contraceptive methods is only one of the requirements for an effective family planning programme. Individuals also need to have complete and accurate information about contraception, including both the benefits and the risks of each method; they need access to follow-up services; and they may need information about and help with other elements of reproductive health. Improving the quality of care, taking into account the client's viewpoint in service design and evaluation, and integrating family planning with other health services are areas needing increased attention.

151. Most family planning clients are women. There is increasing interest in engaging men as clients and in involving women in much larger numbers at the planning and managerial levels of programmes, as well as in service delivery. Both moves have the primary aim of increasing the effectiveness of family planning programmes. Involving women as providers and managers of the programmes may help female clients feel more comfortable and understood, thereby increasing their involvement. It would also have the added benefit of achieving social equity, by opening up professional opportunities for women. Alternatively, increasing the involvement of men in family planning programmes could also be seen as a positive move towards equality through shared responsibility, in addition to helping Governments reach population growth targets. There is a danger, however, in the suggestion that the responsibility for deciding family size should be shifted to the male as the decision maker in the family, in order to ensure that population growth targets are met. In effect, this would counter social equity gains made when women are empowered through broadening their options in life beyond childbearing.

152. It is estimated that over 80 per cent of the users of modern contraception receive their supplies and services from public-sector programmes, most of which provide services and supplies of at least certain contraceptive methods free of charge or at a heavily subsidized price. Reliance on public services tends to be heaviest in Asia, although the public sector is a major

TABLE 11.   AVAILABILITY OF CONTRACEPTIVE SERVICES IN DEVELOPING COUNTRIES, BY REGION, 1982 AND 1989

		Contraceptive availability score (percentage of maximum)[a]		Percentage of population with easy access to								
				Sterilization				IUD		Pill		Condom	
				Female		Male							
Region	Number of countries	1982	1989	1982	1989	1982	1989	1982	1989	1982	1989	1982	1989
All developing countries[b]	89	61	76	56	66	52	58	49	63	42	69	61	71
Africa	40	13	29	5	13	1	3	11	27	17	38	17	39
Northern Africa	6	26	44	7	24	0	0	28	53	38	62	32	47
Other Africa	34	8	25	4	9	1	4	6	19	11	31	12	36
Asia	28	72	86	66	77	66	73	58	72	44	73	69	75
Western Asia	9	11	36	2	14	0	5	8	39	16	46	19	42
Other Asia	19	74	88	69	79	69	76	60	74	45	75	71	77
Excluding China	18	60	79	54	72	54	66	40	63	35	64	59	68
Latin America	20	59	74	56	70	21	32	39	47	65	86	61	87

Sources: Tabulated at the Population Division of the Department for Economic and Social Information and Policy Analysis of the United Nations Secretariat and from family planning availability scores in Robert Sendek and Yvette Bayoumy, "Population Council Databank" (version 3.0). Based on country-specific estimates for 1982 by Robert J. Lapham and W. Parker Mauldin, "Family planning program effort and birth rate decline in developing countries", *International Family Planning Perspectives* (New York), vol. 10. No. 4 (December 1984). pp. 109-118; and for 1989 by W. Parker Mauldin and John A. Ross, "Family planning programs: efforts and results. 1982-1989". Working paper No. 34 (New York. The Population Council. 1991).

NOTES: For countries with estimates available at both dates. These countries contain 97 per cent of the population of developing countries. In order to obtain regional averages. countries have been weighted by population size.

The percentage available was scored on a scale ranging from 0 per cent to 80+ per cent. For countries assigned the maximum score for a particular method. it has been assumed here that 90 per cent of the population had easy access to the method.

[a] The percentage availability represents the sum of the scores for the specific contraceptive methods. The maximum possible score is achieved when all of the specific contraceptive methods shown were judged to be easily available to at least 80 per cent of the population.

[b] Includes one country in Oceania.

source of services in all regions. In some countries, particularly in Latin America, not-for-profit non-governmental organizations are also major suppliers of subsidized services.

Financial resources

153.   One aspect of programme financing that has received increased attention lately is the growing difficulty of paying for the contraceptives themselves. Contraceptive commodities account for an important part of donor assistance, although the greatest portion of the cost is borne by developing-country Governments, which in 1990 paid for approximately 60 per cent of the contraceptive commodities used in the developing countries. UNFPA projects that the annual cost of contraceptive commodities in developing countries will increase by almost 60 per cent between 1990 and 2000, based on current prices, in order to meet the needs of the growing number of couples of child-bearing age and the projected continuing increase in contraceptive prevalence (UNFPA, 1992). Although new and improved methods, such as the Norplant hormonal implant, offer important advantages to users, there is a serious risk that the relatively high cost of such methods will deter developing-country programmes from promoting their introduction on a wide scale.

154.   It is unclear how the rising costs of programmes can be met. Governments will find it difficult even to maintain their current share of costs into the future, particularly considering that the expansion of the number of couples and individuals needing services will occur disproportionately in poor countries. Other possibilities include increasing international donor support, expanding local production of contraceptives in selected countries, and exploring the possibilities for reducing the level of subsidy—through contraceptive social marketing and public sector cost-recovery. To promote cost-sharing, Governments must have better information on the effects of price changes on use. Care must be taken to ensure that those living in poverty, in particular, have access to the services they need.

Issue No. 13.   Adolescents

155.   More than 50 per cent of the world population is under age 25, and 80 per cent of the 1.5 billion young people aged 10-24 years live in developing countries. Furthermore, social conditions in those countries are changing rapidly, and the opportunities for young people to become productive and fully integrated into society are becoming very much restricted. Urbanization, the extension of education, the explosion of telecommunications and the strains on family functioning influence the behaviour adopted by adolescents throughout the world, which will likely persist throughout adulthood.

156.   Concern about the sexual behaviour of adolescents continues to increase as the recognition of the health, population and socio-economic consequences of precocious pregnancy and sexually transmitted diseases, including HIV/AIDS, becomes widespread. The practice of female genital mutilation in some parts of the world is a matter of increasing concern. Since it poses

a major lifelong threat to women's health, it is a form of violence against women that constitutes a violation of basic rights. Although there is a paucity of reliable information about sexual behaviour, some decline in the age-specific fertility rates of women aged under 20 years has been observed in some, but not all, regions. However, indications that abortions are increasingly becoming the main response to unwanted pregnancies and the high prevalence of sexually transmitted diseases among young people demonstrate that unprotected sexual activity is taking place. At the same time, a belief in the social desirability of early marriage and early child-bearing continues to prevail in many countries.

157. Although fertility levels have been decreasing in many regions of the world, the fertility rates of adolescents are very high and in some cases are even increasing. At present, it is estimated that close to 15 million infants born per annum (10 per cent of the total births) are to adolescent mothers. Interest in adolescent health is evident in the increasing number of Governments that are formulating policies to improve programmes and of non-governmental organizations that are initiating activities, often focusing on reproductive health, consistent with the recommendations of the World Population Plan of Action. However, these actions have remained much too limited in scope and coverage to have had significant impact on adolescent reproductive behaviour. The recent Expert Group Meetings on Population and Women (United Nations, 1993d) and on Family Planning, Health and Family Well-being (United Nations, 1993e), convened in preparation for the International Conference on Population and Development, strongly recommended that Governments strengthen programmes so as to provide adolescents of both sexes with the information and means of preventing high-risk pregnancies and births and to protect themselves from sexually transmitted diseases, including HIV/AIDS.

158. Certain obstacles to the prevention of pregnancy and sexually transmitted diseases among young people persist. The first is the inadequacy and inconsistency of policies and legislation curbing early marriage and facilitating the provision of reproductive health services. In order for policies to reflect public concern and support for the healthy development of adolescents, increased advocacy is required in most countries, based on sound information on the health needs of young people and existing responses in each country. Often, policy provisions do not specifically address adolescent needs or there is confusion among community leaders, professionals and adolescents about legislation affecting the health and behaviour of adolescents and its application. A second factor is insufficient knowledge about the sexual and fertility behaviour of adolescents, especially in the developing countries. Such knowledge is important in order to overcome myths about adolescent behaviour and to assist programme design. A third factor is the scant provision of information, education and counselling on family planning, maternity, and the prevention and control of sexually transmitted diseases which focuses on adolescents' needs and their efforts to seek help. Frequently, there are legal and social barriers to using the existing services that are often launched by individuals without sufficient understanding of adolescent development or skills that encourage communication.

159. Recognition of the above barriers is implicit in the Plan of Action and the Mexico City recommendations, and concentrated efforts are required in the future to secure their adequate implementation and thus ensure improved reproductive health among adolescents.

---

[1]The estimates of contraceptive availability are approximate, based on country-specific estimates provided by knowledgeable observers. See *World Population Monitoring, 1993* (United Nations, 1995b).

VII. HEALTH AND MORTALITY

160. Recent mortality declines can be attributed to advancements in health technology and to socio-economic development, particularly as expressed in improved living standards, better nutrition, increased education and the improved status of women. Longevity has intrinsic value, since it allows people to achieve their goals and aspirations. This chapter focuses on maternal mortality and the demographic impact of AIDS as well as on the goals and targets specified in the World Population Plan of Action.

Issue No. 14. Goals and targets in morbidity and mortality

Levels, trends and prospects of mortality

161. Mortality levels, trends and prospects are assessed through three indicators:

(*a*) Life expectancy at birth (the expected average number of years to be lived by a person newly born, assuming a fixed schedule of age-specific mortality rates);

(*b*) The infant mortality rate (the number of deaths per 1,000 live births between birth and exact age 1);

(*c*) Mortality of children under age 5, also called the under-5 mortality rate (the number of deaths per 1,000 live births between birth and exact age 5).

Table 12 presents numerical information on these three mortality indicators worldwide. Maternal mortality is discussed separately in paragraphs 181-195 below.

162. The trends in life expectancy, infant mortality and under-five mortality that are briefly presented here reflect the different phases of an epidemiological transition. According to estimates from WHO, infectious and parasitic diseases account for almost half of all deaths and remain the leading cause of mortality in the developing countries (45 per cent of the deaths, compared with only 4.7 per cent in the developed countries). More than 2 billion people living in about 100 countries are currently exposed to malaria, which has manifested an upward trend in some Latin American and Asian countries. Schistosomiasis is also endemic in 76 countries, where about 200 million people are reported to be infected. It is estimated that in 1990 some 1.7 billion people around the world were infected by tuberculosis and that more than 20 million were suffering from the disease, 95 per cent of whom were living in the developing countries. In the developed countries, cardiovascular diseases are the leading cause of morbidity and mortality, followed by cancer and malignant neoplasms. More recently, tuberculosis has made a powerful comeback in some developed countries, particularly among the underprivileged.

TABLE 12. MORTALITY INDICATORS, 1950-2015

Region	Life expectancy at birth (years)			Infant mortality rate (per 1,000 births)			Under-five mortality rate (per 1,000 births)		
	1950-1955	1990-1995	2010-2015	1950-1955	1990-1995	2010-2015	1950-1955	1990-1995	2010-2015
World..................	46.4	64.4	69.9	156	64	40	240	83	57
More developed countries...........	66.5	74.4	77.3	59	10	7	73	14	10
Less developed countries...........	40.9	62.3	68.4	179	70	44	281	106	64
Least developed countries...........	35.7	51.2	59.3	194	110	73	..	..	..

Source: World Population Prospects: The 1994 Revision (United Nations publication, Sales No. E.95.XIII.16).

Life expectancy at birth

163. At the world level, for the quinquennium 1990-1995, life expectancy at birth is estimated at 64.7 years (62.7 for males and 66.7 for females), representing an increase of 41 per cent from the figure of 46.4 years estimated for the period 1950-1955. A large proportion of that increase took place during the 1950s and early 1960s, and a slow-down was recorded during the 1970s. The medium-variant projections indicate a life expectancy of 70 years in 2010-2015 (68 for males and 72.5 for females).[1]

164. In 1950-1955, the gap in life expectancy between the more developed and the less developed regions was about 25 years. Since then, improvements in mortality have been more rapid in the less developed regions, so that by 1992 that difference had narrowed to 12 years. In fact, the more developed regions have passed from a life expectancy of 66.5 years in 1950-1955 (63.9 for males and 69.0 for females) to a current life expectancy of 74.4 years (70.6 for males and 78.1 for females) in 1990-1995, and the figure is projected to reach 77.3 years in 2010-2015 (74.0 for males and 80.8 for females). Currently, Japan has the highest life expectancy, 79.5 years (76.4 for males and 82.5 for females).

165. Compared with the current level of life expectancy in the more developed regions (about 70-77 years), the range of levels in the less developed regions is large—from 49 years in Eastern Africa to 72 years in Eastern Asia. In most of Africa, life expectancy is about 53 years; in Asia, 65 years; and in Latin America, 68 years. In all the countries of Eastern Asia, except Mongolia, life expectancy is currently over 70 years.

166. Sub-Saharan Africa continues to have the highest level of mortality in the world. The impressive mortality declines that occurred in other regions of the developing world with the introduction of health interventions that reduced mortality caused by infectious and parasitic diseases have not yet been realized in sub-Saharan Africa. Although the AIDS pandemic is dealt with below as a separate issue, it is important to mention here that it is particularly severe in Eastern Africa, Middle Africa and Western Africa, and that it has further compromised any effort at improving life expectancy. In the particu-

lar case of Uganda, for example, it is estimated that in the absence of AIDS, the current life expectancy of 41.8 years (40.8 for males and 42.9 for females) would have been 50 years.

Infant mortality and under-five mortality

167.   There have been important improvements in the infant mortality rate for the world. It declined from 156 deaths per 1,000 live births in 1950-1955 to the current figure of 64 per 1,000 in 1990-1995, and it is projected to reach 40 per 1,000 in 2010-2015. A similar picture can be obtained by observing the evolution of the under-five mortality rate, which dropped from 240 per 1,000 births in 1950-1955 to the current value of 83 per 1,000; it is projected to decline to 57 per 1,000 in 2010-2015. Nevertheless, behind such spectacular achievements there are wide disparities among regions, countries and provinces, and by gender.

168.   With regard to infant mortality, there has been a significant reduction in the gap between the developed and the developing countries. Infant mortality in the more developed regions fell from 56 per 1,000 births in 1950-1955 to the current level of 12 per 1,000, and is projected to decline to 8 per 1,000 in 2010-2015. From 179 per 1,000 in 1950-1955, the infant mortality rate in the less developed regions is currently estimated to have declined to 70 per 1,000, and it is projected to reach 44 per 1,000 in 2010-2015. Similar dramatic declines can also be observed in terms of under-five mortality. From 240 per 1,000 in 1950-1955, the under-five mortality rate for the world has declined to a current value of 83 per 1,000 and is projected to be 57 per 1,000 in 2010-2015.

169.   It is important to note the increasing sex differential in life expectancy at birth: the number of additional years of life expectancy enjoyed by women compared with men rose in the more developed regions from 5.3 years four decades ago to 7 years currently. A similar pattern can be observed in the less developed regions, where the gap between female and male life expectancy increased from 1.5 to 2.8 years during the same period. Various reasons have been advanced to explain these differences. One is genetic: the protective effect of women's endogenous sex hormones may reduce their risk of having ischemic heart disease. It has also been hypothesized that social and cultural environmental factors have hindered women from engaging in behaviour that is dangerous to one's health, such as substance abuse, risk-taking and hazardous employment. However, in some European countries there is a clear indication that increased smoking among women has contributed to a narrowing in the gap in life expectancy. None the less, not all behavioural changes are necessarily harmful. Current evidence suggests that, on average, the increased acceptability of women's employment outside the home has not been harmful to their health or contributed to a decrease in life expectancy at birth.

Policies aimed at reducing mortality

170.   Despite the availability of modern technologies, the major obstacle to improving health conditions in the developing countries is the weak-

ness of the health infrastructure and the lack of adequate human resources. Infectious and parasitic diseases continue to pose serious risks to child and adult health in the developing countries. Although gaps between the developing and the developed countries have been significantly reduced, particularly in relation to mortality levels, it is important to emphasize that improved levels of survival do not necessarily mean that the population is enjoying better health conditions. More effort is required to increase awareness, at all levels, about the important contribution that primary health care can make to the process of development and to the fact that universal access to such services is of high priority.

Life expectancy at birth and infant mortality

171. The Plan of Action set explicit quantitative targets for reductions in the levels of mortality, indicating that the world as a whole should achieve a life expectancy at birth of 62 years by 1985 and of 74 years by 2000 (para. 22). These figures have often been cited as implicit goals for mortality improvement at the regional level as well. It is possible only now to verify whether the target that the Plan of Action set for 1985 has been reached, since the data needed to estimate mortality levels during the 1980s for a large number of developing countries were not available earlier. At the world level, although life expectancy was estimated to have just met the target of 62 years set for 1985, it is expected to fall short of the target of 74 years set for the year 2000. (The projected value is 67.5 for 2000-2005.) In the less developed regions as a whole, although impressive gains in survivorship have been made, life expectancy fell short of the target for 1985 by two years.

172. In 1985, none of the subregions in Africa met the target life expectancy. In Asia, the situation was mixed. Eastern Asia and Western Asia exceeded the target, but Southern Asia lagged by six years and South-eastern Asia, by two years. Life expectancy in all the Latin American subregions, however, exceeded the target by at least five years. In general, recent trends support the conclusion that no developing region is expected to reach the target set for the year 2000. In the more developed regions, Eastern Europe and the former USSR are expected to reach life expectancies of 73 and 72 years, respectively, by the year 2000 (still falling short of the target of 74 years).

173. The Plan of Action also set targets for countries with the highest mortality levels: by 1985 they should have reached a life expectancy at birth of at least 50 years and an infant mortality rate of less than 120 deaths per 1,000 live births (para. 23). Mexico City recommendation 14 revised the targets for the year 2000 and proposed that countries with higher mortality levels should aim for a life expectancy at birth of at least 60 years and an infant mortality rate of less than 50 per 1,000 live births and that countries with intermediate mortality levels should aim for a life expectancy at birth of at least 70 years and an infant mortality rate of less than 35 per 1,000 live births.

174. According to *World Population Prospects: The 1994 Revision*, none of the regions of Africa and fewer than half of the African countries met the target for life expectancy set by the Plan of Action for 1985; fewer than

half met the target for infant mortality. Projections to the year 2000 suggest that an even greater number of countries in Africa are unlikely to meet the targets for either life expectancy or infant mortality set for that year. However, four countries (Cape Verde, Mauritius, Réunion and Tunisia) are expected to meet the targets (for both life expectancy and infant mortality) set for countries with intermediate levels of mortality.

175. In Asia, six countries (three in South-eastern Asia, two in Southern Asia and one in Western Asia) did not meet the targets for life expectancy and infant mortality for 1985. Bangladesh just met the target for life expectancy but fell short of the target for infant mortality. The same six countries are not expected to reach a life expectancy of 60 years and infant mortality of less than 50 per 1,000 live births by the year 2000. An additional six countries (mostly in Southern Asia) are not expected to meet the target for infant mortality, although life expectancy is expected to be above 60 years by the year 2000. The targets set for countries with intermediate levels of mortality are likely to be met by 23 countries in Asia, including all of Eastern Asia (except Mongolia), Western Asia (except Yemen and Iraq), 6 countries in South-eastern Asia and 2 countries in Southern Asia. The Philippines and Viet Nam are expected to reach the target for infant mortality, although their life expectancy levels may fall short of the target.

176. In Oceania, the 1985 target was met by all countries, and by the year 2000, it is expected that only Papua New Guinea will not meet the target set for countries with intermediate levels of mortality. All of the Latin American countries met the infant mortality goals and exceeded the 1985 target for life expectancy by at least five years. By the year 2000, of the 28 countries with intermediate levels of mortality in Latin America, 17 are expected to meet the targets for life expectancy and infant mortality; only Haiti is not expected to reach either target.

177. The Programme of Action, adopted at Cairo, in 1994, recommends that all countries should make access to basic health care and health promotion the central strategies for mortality reduction in the next 20 years. To that end, the Programme of Action suggests new actions that can be taken to strengthen basic health-care services. In addition, it recommends reform of the health sector and greater cost-effectiveness in health programmes. It also sets new time-bound goals for countries to improve their life expectancy at birth. Furthermore, it recognizes the role of women as the primary custodians of family health and encourages supporting that role through expanded health education, making available simple cost-effective remedies and reappraising primary health-care services. Moreover, it specifies the areas in which Governments should seek community participation in health-policy planning, in particular with respect to the long-term care of the elderly, those with disabilities and those infected with HIV and other endemic diseases.

178. Regarding the accessibility to generic drugs and vaccines, the Programme of Action recommends that the international community should facilitate the transfer to developing countries of technology for local manufacture, quality control and distribution. The Programme of Action supports previous recommendations concerning the promotion of environmental and

occupational health but further suggests the regular monitoring of the impact of environmental problems on the health of vulnerable groups.

Mortality of children under age 5

179. The Plan of Action recommended, as one of its priorities, a reduction in child mortality (recommendation 24 (*a*)). This goal was reaffirmed by Governments at the 1990 World Summit for Children. Through improvements in immunization coverage (the goal of 80 per cent immunization coverage was reached in 1990), oral rehydration therapy and basic sanitation, important progress has been made in the reduction of deaths of children under age 5. Child death rates have been halved in almost every region of the developing world (except in sub-Saharan Africa) since at least 1960. There has been a decrease not only in the rates of child deaths but also in the absolute numbers. (The annual number of under-five deaths was close to 20 million in the early 1950s but declined to about 15 million in 1980-1985 and is currently estimated to be close to 13 million.)

180. The eighth WHO report on the world health situation[2] indicates that in countries where the prevalence of infectious and parasitic diseases is high, about one half of all deaths typically occur before age 5. Most of the infant and under-five morbidity and mortality, however, could be prevented through the provision of adequate water supply and sanitation facilities at the community level. For that reason, the International Conference on Population, which took place in the middle of the International Drinking Water Supply and Sanitation Decade, urged the provision of a sufficient supply of potable water and adequate sanitation facilities for the eradication or control of infectious and parasitic diseases (recommendation 22). However, while the percentage of the population in need of essential services increased during that same decade, millions of individuals remain without access to water and sanitation services, because services have not kept pace with the increases in population.

Issue No. 15. Maternal mortality

181. Maternal mortality is one of the leading causes of death among women in their reproductive years in the developing world. However, it was not until recently that the magnitude of the problem was recognized, thanks to the growing number of surveys that make it possible to estimate maternal mortality rates when they cannot be derived from civil registration sources. Maternal mortality is measured as the annual number of deaths of women related to pregnancy and childbirth per 100,000 births.

182. The main causes of maternal death are haemorrhage, infection, toxaemia and obstructed labour. Studies have shown that the factors that contribute to high maternal mortality in the developing countries include the relatively large number of pregnancies among women at the extremes of the childbearing range (maternal mortality rates for women below the age of 20 are 5-7 times higher than those of women aged 20-24 years, in some countries), maternal depletion through pregnancies that are too closely spaced, and the high prevalence of high-parity births. The risk of death related to pregnancy

is further exacerbated if women are poor, malnourished, uneducated or beyond the reach of adequate health care. In the developing countries, complications resulting from poorly performed abortions, as was indicated above, account for a significant proportion of maternal deaths, estimated at about 30 per cent.

Levels, trends and prospects

183.   Of the demographic and health variables, maternal mortality is the indicator that exhibits the widest disparity among countries. On the basis of data tabulated by WHO, it has been estimated that at least half a million women die from causes related to pregnancy and childbirth each year. All but about 4,000 of those deaths take place in developing countries. The incidence of maternal mortality ranges from almost non-existent (Iceland reported only one maternal death in 1987 and one in 1990, Malta has had none since 1986 nor has Finland since 1989) to very high (above 1,000 deaths per 100,000 births in some rural areas of Africa). Scattered information suggests that in some countries, one fourth to one half of all the deaths of women of childbearing age result from pregnancy and its complications. The risks associated with pregnancy and childbirth seem, at the global level, to be about 5 per cent lower than they were five years ago. However, because the number of births increased by some 7 per cent over the same period, the total number of maternal deaths has remained almost unchanged.

184.   In a majority of the developed countries, maternal mortality rates, registered recently, were below 10 deaths per 100,000 live births (rates below 4 per 100,000 are common in Northern European countries) and only in Hungary, Romania and the former USSR was the rate above 20. In Romania, the maternal mortality rate in 1990 was 83 per 100,000 live births. According to WHO estimates, the maternal mortality rate for developed countries in the aggregate declined from 30 to 26 per 100,000 live births between 1983 and 1988. Reaching and maintaining low levels of maternal mortality have been significant achievements in public health in the developed world. Advancements in obstetric and prenatal care, the introduction of antibiotics and blood transfusions, the increasing proportion of deliveries taking place in hospitals, and the better general health and nutritional status of pregnant women, along with the introduction of effective means of contraception and the provision of safe abortion, have all been important factors in the reduction of maternal mortality in the developed countries.

185.   In contrast, the estimated maternal mortality rate for the less developed regions was, around 1988, 420 deaths per 100,000 births, a figure that was about 5 per cent lower than it had been five years earlier. For the group of least developed countries, the rates are estimated at about 700 per 100,000 live births. Although data on maternal mortality are still very scanty, WHO has estimated that Africa has the highest rate (630 per 100,000 births), followed by Asia (380) and Latin America (200).

186.   Comparing new information on maternal mortality with that available five years ago suggests that pregnancy and childbirth have become somewhat safer for women in most of Asia and in parts of Latin America. In con-

trast, the situation has changed very little in most parts of sub-Saharan Africa, where the increase in the number of births has led to a parallel increase in the number of maternal deaths. In addition, there may have been an increase in the risk of maternal mortality itself. However, it is not immediately apparent which of the changes mentioned in this paragraph and paragraph 164 are real and which are due to better information having become available in the meantime. The situation there is the worst in the world and reflects the deteriorating economic and health conditions in the sub-Saharan region.

Policies aimed at reducing maternal mortality

187.   The Plan of Action calls for national and international efforts to reduce general morbidity and mortality and for particularly vigorous efforts to reduce foetal, infant and early childhood mortality and related maternal morbidity and mortality (para. 24 (*a*)). Mexico City (recommendation 18 (*b*)-(*g*)) adopted more precise guidelines to achieve this goal and urged action in relation to prenuptial medical examinations; prenatal and perinatal care, with special attention to high-risk pregnancies, and safe delivery by trained attendants; the nutritional needs of pregnant women; avoidance of abortion and the provision of humane treatment and counselling of women who have had abortions; access to family planning for preventing high-risk pregnancies; and education to change attitudes about early child-bearing. The Mexico City recommendations also set the goal of reducing maternal mortality by at least half by the year 2000 in countries where it was higher than 100 maternal deaths per 100,000 births (recommendation 18(*a*)). The Economic and Social Council, in its resolution 1989/92, after discussing the results of the third review and appraisal conducted in 1989, urged Governments and international organizations to strengthen their efforts to achieve the targets established by the International Conference on Population for the reduction of mortality in general and child and maternal mortality in particular; it also identified many of the factors associated with high levels of maternal mortality: pregnancies in the youngest and oldest reproductive age groups; pregnancies too closely spaced; high-parity births; lack of access to health services; lack of trained birth attendants; and the complications resulting from unsafe abortions (United Nations, 1989b).

188.   In the eight years since the goal of reducing high maternal mortality by 50 per cent per annum by the year 2000 was formulated at the International Safe Motherhood Conference (World Bank, 1987), many countries have formally endorsed it. Most countries with high maternal mortality have also implemented various action plans to deal with the problem. In addition, as an indication of the continued commitment to dealing with high maternal mortality, the goal was reaffirmed in the Goals for Children and Development in the 1990s,[3] which have been accepted by the great majority of countries.

189.   In 1987, WHO, along with four other United Nations organizations and two non-governmental organizations (the United Nations Development Programme (UNDP), UNFPA, the United Nations Children's Fund (UNICEF), the World Bank, the International Planned Parenthood Federation

(IPPF) and the Population Council), agreed to collaborate in a safe motherhood initiative. An inter-agency group set up for the purpose of coordinating efforts to reduce maternal mortality has been meeting biannually since then. At the group's meeting in November 1992, the member agencies and organizations committed themselves to intensifying their efforts and further improving the coordination of their activities. Several other non-governmental organizations have joined the inter-agency group—among them Family Health International (United States), which has recently established a department of maternal and neonatal health; Santé maternelle internationale (International maternal health) (France); and Family Care International (United States). Many other organizations contribute to the reduction of maternal mortality by promoting family planning and reproductive health around the world.

190. A number of bilateral agencies have joined the effort to reduce the unacceptably high number of maternal deaths. The Governments of Australia, Denmark, France, Germany, Italy, Japan, the Netherlands, Norway, Sweden, the United Kingdom of Great Britain and Northern Ireland and the United States, to name a few, have provided funds and/or technical cooperation to developing countries for the improvement of maternal health. Those Governments also exchange information with the inter-agency group.

191. It has been established in some countries that increased provision and improvement of existing maternity services at all levels of the health system is the most effective means of reducing maternal mortality. Family planning programmes, together with good primary health care are also important interventions for achieving reductions in maternal mortality. The efficacy of such programmes would be greatly enhanced by the inclusion of safe and readily accessible contraceptive methods, and, where appropriate, access to safe abortion services.

192. Most of the above-mentioned Governments, agencies and organizations are cooperating with countries that have demonstrated a strong political will to assess maternal health needs; develop national plans of action (which are part of, or integrated with, the overall national health plan) aimed at meeting the assessed needs; and implement the plans of action as quickly and efficiently as possible. This process has begun or is being initiated in Bangladesh, Bolivia, Guinea, Indonesia, the Philippines, Senegal and the United Republic of Tanzania, to name a few. Guidelines now being written on safe motherhood programme development and implementation include standards for maternal health services delivery and management. As countries proceed to develop and implement national strategies, those guidelines will prove invaluable.

193. In spite of these aggressive efforts to reduce maternal mortality, the total number of maternal deaths worldwide has not yet started to decrease. This suggests that the implementation of the recommendations of the Plan of Action had a slower start than anticipated. This may have been due partly to competition for scarce resources, compounded by global recession and the emergence of other crises, such as overwhelming famine and the AIDS pandemic which have required large sums of financial aid, and partly to lack of a sense of urgency on the part of many countries and agencies about acting

aggressively enough at the beginning. The lack of a sense of urgency has been largely overcome by the information and advocacy efforts of Governments and certain agencies, but the problem of restricted resources has not abated and can be expected to continue for the foreseeable future.

194. Another difficulty has been the size and multisectoral nature of the problem of maternal mortality. The approach used until recently by most agencies was to develop discrete, time-limited, self-contained projects. This has proved completely inadequate for dealing with such a complex problem. To make motherhood safer requires a massive and simultaneous attack on all the elements contributing to the problem, including the deficiencies of the health sector, education, legislation, social services, and the rights of women. In the health sector alone, the entire infrastructure of the health system needs strengthening in most countries where maternal mortality is high. This means building new structures, renovating existing ones, providing equipment and supplies, training personnel, and improving management and supervision practices, among other things.

195. Broad vision is required on the part of planners, and concerted, integrated efforts must be made by Governments, funding agencies and technical cooperation organizations. Efficient methods for planning safe motherhood programmes are of recent origin. Previous instructions were imprecise and did not provide guidance in pointing the way for countries desiring to start the process. In addition, coordination of the activities of a large number of agencies is difficult at best and many agencies are only beginning to identify ways of working effectively with others. All these obstacles have delayed the building up of the necessary momentum to reduce maternal mortality. However, early indicators now suggest that many of those obstacles have been or are being overcome, and momentum is building up.

Issue No. 16. Acquired immunodeficiency syndrome (AIDS)

196. The World Population Plan of Action (para. 24 (*e*)) recognized the adverse effect of poor health on working-age populations and their productivity. Although HIV, the causal agent for AIDS, had not even been identified in 1974, the long latency period for this virus indicates that it had already started spreading in the 1970s. Still, when the HIV virus was identified in the early 1980s, its deadly effects were limited. Perhaps for that reason, the Mexico City recommendations did not make specific reference to what has now become a devastating epidemic that threatens to undermine major gains in the reduction of morbidity and mortality in both developed and developing countries. This virus has spread most rapidly among adults in their prime, resulting in the loss of a valuable resource to families, communities and countries. In addition, the number of infants born with HIV infection has been increasing and threatens to jeopardize gains in child survival anticipated from immunization programmes and other child-health initiatives. Moreover, the enormous cost of caring for the rising number of AIDS patients have already started taxing the resources of health-care systems and raising concerns that diverting resources from other health programmes could have adverse consequences for future improvements in overall survivorship. Given the magnitude of the AIDS pan-

demic, its substantial negative effects on social organization and economic development are already being felt in some countries, threatening the implementation of the World Population Plan of Action and Mexico City recommendations 19, 22 and 23. Finally, projections show that the epidemic is expected to worsen in the 1990s so that efforts to combat AIDS need to be explicitly articulated.

Levels, trends and prospects

197. In a December 1994 press release, WHO estimated that well over 17 million men, women and children had been infected with HIV since the start of the pandemic and at least 4 million individuals had developed AIDS. The total number of infected individuals has increased by 3 million since mid-1993 and is projected to reach 30 million–40 million by the year 2000. In addition, it is estimated that over half a million children have been infected with HIV from their infected mothers and that 5 million–10 million children will be orphaned by AIDS by the year 2000. The epidemic incapacitates people at the ages when they are most needed for the support of the young and the elderly.

198. The majority of the world's HIV cases have resulted from infection through heterosexual transmission, which together with homosexual transmission accounts for about three quarters of HIV infections worldwide. Two other modes of transmission of this infection are through blood and blood products, from transfusions, and injections of infected blood; and from mother to child, including both perinatal and post-partum transmission. Virtually all persons diagnosed as having AIDS die within a few years. In infants born infected with HIV, the progression to AIDS is more rapid than in adults. Survival after diagnosis has been increasing in the developed countries from an average of less than one year to between one and two years at present. However, survival after the onset of AIDS in the developing countries remains short—an estimated six months or less. Longer survival periods seem to be directly related to the routine use of antiviral and prophylactic drugs and a better overall quality of health care.

199. The AIDS epidemic has been most devastating in sub-Saharan Africa. WHO estimated that by 1992, 1.5 million adults in the region would develop AIDS and more than 7 million would be infected with HIV. In that region, HIV transmission has been predominantly through heterosexual relations; and in the infected population, men and women account for nearly equal proportions. Since many women of child-bearing age are infected, HIV transmission from an infected woman to her child before, during or shortly after birth is widespread and a growing problem in the region. This epidemic may bring to a halt future improvements in survivorship for some countries in Africa. In the 15 countries of Eastern, Central and Western Africa where the proportion of those infected was above 1 per cent in the adult population in 1990, the already low level of life expectancy at birth (of about 50 years in 1985-1990) is projected to remain unchanged through the year 2000. AIDS is likely to cause an additional annual 2.9 deaths per 1,000 population in those countries by 1995-2000. Because as many women as men carry the virus, WHO

estimates that child mortality may increase by as much as 50 per cent through mother-to-child transmission in much of sub-Saharan Africa during the 1990s, thereby offsetting gains in child survival achieved over the past two decades, as in Mexico City recommendation 17.

200. Initially, transmission of HIV in Northern America, Europe and Australia occurred predominantly through homosexual contact. Increasingly, the virus has been spreading among intravenous drug users and heterosexuals, especially in Northern America. WHO estimates that 1.6 million cases of HIV infection might have occurred in those regions as of 1992 (about two thirds of them in the United States) and that close to 350,000 or more cases of AIDS may have occurred by that time. It is expected that through the 1990s, homosexual men and intravenous drug users will continue to be the population groups most affected by AIDS in the above-mentioned regions, but new infections will occur predominantly in heterosexual men and women having multiple sex partners.

201. As for Latin America, the transmission of HIV in the early stages occurred through heterosexual and bisexual men and intravenous drug users. Since the mid-1980s, heterosexual transmission, initially introduced to the population by bisexual men transmitting HIV to their female partners, has become more important. The Caribbean and the urban areas of Brazil are the worst affected. It is estimated that currently about 1 million people in the region may be infected with HIV.

202. The AIDS epidemic took hold in Asia in the second half of the 1980s. Initially, injecting drug users constituted the group most affected, but heterosexual transmission has been increasing and is now the predominant mode of transmission. Currently, India and Thailand are the countries worst affected. Estimates of the size of the HIV-infected population are not available for the region as a whole but in India, as of mid-1992, the estimate was up to 1 million and in Thailand, about 400,000.

Action and policies

203. WHO established a global programme on AIDS at the beginning of 1987. By 1990, more than 150 countries had established national AIDS committees to coordinate national control programmes. The Global Strategy for the Prevention and Control of AIDS (known as the Global AIDS Strategy) was initially drawn up by WHO in 1985-1986 and unanimously approved by the fortieth World Health Assembly (May 1987), and the Venice Summit of the Heads of State or Government (June 1987). Since that time, it has served as the main policy framework for the global response to the pandemic, and it is directed and coordinated by WHO in keeping with its mandate from the General Assembly (resolution 43/15). The Strategy calls for direct action and research to lessen the impact of AIDS and, in particular, to reduce the burden on women, who often carry primary responsibility for providing AIDS care. The Strategy was revised in 1991 and endorsed by the World Health Assembly and the General Assembly in 1992. While the three main objectives of the Strategy remain the same (namely, to prevent infection with HIV, reduce the personal and social impact of HIV infection, and mobilize and unify national

and international efforts against AIDS), the revised version reflects the new challenges of the evolving pandemic. These include:

(*a*)   Increased emphasis on care;

(*b*)   Better treatment for other sexually transmitted diseases;

(*c*)   Greater focus on HIV prevention through improvement of women's health, educational, legal and social status;

(*d*)   A more supportive environment for prevention programmes;

(*e*)   Provision for the socio-economic impact of the pandemic; and

(*f*)   Greater emphasis on explaining the public health dangers of stigmatization and discrimination.

204.   The Global AIDS Strategy outlines various approaches to overcoming official denial of the existence of HIV infection by national authorities and complacency about its current and expected magnitude and the attitudes reflected in the general public. Another challenge is discrimination against individuals with HIV/AIDS, an irrational response which often stems from the stigma attached to sexually transmitted diseases and mistaken belief that HIV can be transmitted through casual social contact. Non-discrimination is thus vital, not only for the sake of human rights but also because of its strong public health rationale.

205.   In its policy and intervention development; social, behavioural and biomedical research; and information/education activities, the Global AIDS Strategy pursues a gender-specific approach aimed at benefiting women. It has developed a comprehensive strategy on women and AIDS to guide the development of policies and interventions at both the global and country levels, emphasizing women's physical, social and economic vulnerability to HIV infection and recommending action in each area. In addition, it addresses the need to reduce the social and personal impact on women (including their disproportionate share of care-giving in relation to the pandemic) and the links between reducing HIV infection and developing comprehensive approaches to women's health. Specific reference is made to ensuring women's reproductive rights, including improved access to barrier methods of contraception that prevent both pregnancy and infection from HIV and sexually transmitted diseases, and a wide range of family planning services.

206.   Support is geared above all to the implementation of effective strategies and interventions for prevention and care and to the strengthening of national managerial capacity. A strong management structure is essential for implementing an intersectoral AIDS programme. To enable country programmes to develop as rapidly and as effectively as possible, the programme has developed programme manager training courses for national senior-level staff from various sectors. The courses cover the planning, implementation, monitoring and evaluating of national AIDS programmes. The WHO programme initiates and supports research to identify and develop effective interventions and approaches for the prevention and management of HIV/AIDS. Furthermore, it provides guidance, educational materials and technical assistance to national AIDS programmes and a wide range of other partners in the implementation of approaches and interventions, especially at the country level.

207.   The programme also coordinates, supports and promotes various types of clinical and biomedical research. Key areas of research include vaccine development; clinical research and drug development; diagnostics; and epidemiological research, surveillance and forecasting. Finally, the programme has been actively involved in efforts to improve coordination of HIV/AIDS-related activities at both the global and country levels. This has included the organization of an assessment of coordination of HIV/AIDS activities in six countries (October 1992), the strengthening of the Interagency Advisory Group on AIDS (IAAG), and the establishment of a Task Force on HIV/AIDS Coordination which reports to the programme's Management Committee. Continued attention will be given to this area in the coming years.

208.   In January 1994, the WHO Executive Board recommended the creation of a joint and co-sponsored United Nations programme on HIV/AIDS in order to boost the global response to the pandemic, and by December 1994, a new director for that programme had been selected. This new United Nations programme brings together the AIDS-related activities of six United Nations organizations: UNICEF, UNDP, UNFPA, UNESCO, WHO and the World Bank. The United Nations programme on HIV/AIDS will build on the experience and strength of each co-sponsor. The programme will seek support for a strong, effective and comprehensive global response to the pandemic. At the global level, the joint programme will provide support in policy formulation, strategic planning, technical guidance, research and development, advocacy and external relations. At the country level, the programme will strengthen national capacities to respond to the overall impact of HIV/AIDS. The transition from the efforts of the six participating organizations to one joint and co-sponsored AIDS programme has already begun and is expected to be fully operational by early 1996.

NOTES

[1]The figures on life expectancy at birth and infant mortality rates are taken from *World Population Prospects: The 1994 Revision* (United Nations, 1995a).

[2]*Implementation of the Global Strategy for Health for All by the Year 2000. Second Evaluation* (Geneva, WHO, 1993).

[3]The Goals are contained in the World Declaration on the Survival, Protection and Development of Children and the Plan of Action for Implementing the World Declaration in the 1990s (A/45/473, annex).

VIII. POPULATION DISTRIBUTION, URBANIZATION AND INTERNAL MIGRATION

209. According to current estimates, by the end of the twentieth century, the world will have, for the first time in history, more urban than rural people. This transformation has affected every aspect of human life and accompanied other important social and economic transformations, particularly in the developing countries. Urbanization, or an increase in the proportion of the population living in urban areas, is the result of three major components: migration to the urban areas; areal reclassification; and natural increase in the urban areas. Although it is very difficult to estimate the exact contribution of each of the three components, the figure for urbanization due to internal migration and areal reclassification ranges between 40 and 50 per cent, with the rest due to natural growth.

210. The levels of urbanization are continuing to rise, slowly in the more developed regions and more rapidly in the less developed ones (United Nations, 1995c). In 1990, 43.1 per cent of the world population (2.3 billion people) lived in urban areas (73.6 per cent in the more developed regions and 34.7 in the less developed regions). Such levels are in contrast with those determined in 1950, when 29.3 per cent of the world population lived in urban areas (54.7 per cent in the more developed regions and 17.3 per cent in the less developed regions). It is projected that the proportions will increase to 55.5 per cent by the year 2015. At the same time, urbanization in the less developed regions will climb from 34.7 to 50.5 per cent.

211. Most Governments currently recognize that urbanization is an inevitable and irreversible process and that, as an integral part of economic and social development, it needs to be guided rather than obstructed. There is ample empirical proof that urbanization has many beneficial effects, including the acceleration of economic growth, the improvement of the social and cultural environment, the amelioration of education and health services, the more efficient use of land, and even reductions in fertility rates. It is also being increasingly recognized that voluntary migration is a rational response to spatial inequalities and that urbanization is an intrinsic part of the development process.

212. As the urbanization trend has demonstrated for decades, policies to control the growth of large cities have rarely been successful. According to the information contained in the Population Policy Data Bank, only 7 per cent of national Governments consider their own national population distribution pattern to be satisfactory; 25 per cent regard a minor change as desirable; and 45 per cent believe that a major change is required.

213. It must be borne in mind, however, that the growth of urban agglomerations should be accompanied by an allocation of adequate resources

to cope with the scale of new demands for employment, housing, infrastructure and services. Efficient management based on integrated urban policies is a necessary condition for beneficial exploitation of the potentials of urbanization and minimization effects. Sound rural development policies are equally important since they promote creation of new markets for urban goods and services and at the same time improve the living conditions in rural areas. The role played by intermediate and small cities in supporting rural development should also be recognized. If properly managed, these settlements could, in attracting potential migrants, act as counter-magnets with respect to large urban agglomerations.

Issue No. 17. Population growth in large urban agglomerations

Levels, trends and prospects

214. At the global level, the urban population has been growing steadily throughout the past four decades: it grew from 738 million in 1950 to 2,277 million in 1990, and according to the latest United Nations projections, it is expected to reach 2,926 million by the year 2000 and 4,143 million by the year 2015. While the overall rate of growth of the urban population is gradually decreasing, the rate for the developing countries will remain above 3 per cent per annum up to the year 2005. Most of the urban population increase will occur in the developing countries. During the 1990s, it is estimated that the urban population in the developed countries will increase by approximately 62 million, whereas in the developing countries the increase will be as much as 587 million. How much of this growth occurs in the largest urban agglomerations will depend on how successful developing regions are in restructuring the hierarchy of their urban places.

215. Current trends in the process of urbanization in the developing regions are marked by the concentration of a country's urban population in a single large city (a phenomenon called "primacy"), and by the increasing replacement, by natural population increase in the urban areas, of rural-to-urban migration as the predominant cause of urban growth. Large urban agglomerations have been growing and are continuing to grow in size and number. In 1950 only New York had more than 10 million inhabitants; by 1970 two Asian cities, Tokyo and Shanghai, had grown to be as large. Two decades later, in 1990, 12 urban agglomerations had at least 10 million residents, and the number of such urban agglomerations is projected to be 22 the year 2010. All but one of the new cities are in the less developed regions. Eight of the 12 largest urban agglomerations in 1990 were in the less developed regions; the proportion is expected to increase to 18 out of a total of 22 in the year 2010.

216. With 25 million inhabitants in 1990, Tokyo was by far the largest urban agglomeration in the world, but by 2010, urban agglomerations exceeding a population size of 20 million will have become more common. Bombay (India), Shanghai (China), Lagos (Nigeria) and São Paulo (Brazil) are all projected to have at least 20 million residents in 2010. Table 13 shows the population size at three points in time for the 22 urban agglomerations pro-

jected to exceed 10 million by 2010. Some cities show enormous growth during the 40-year period between 1970 and 2010. Lagos (Nigeria) and Dhaka (Bangladesh), for example, began the time-period with relatively small populations (2.0 million and 1.3 million, respectively), but they are expected to be among the world's 11 largest urban agglomerations by the year 2010. Their annual population growth rates were among the highest in the world in the period 1970-1975, 9.8 per cent and 7.9 per cent, respectively, and they are expected to continue to show rapid growth to the year 2010.

217.   By contrast, urban agglomerations in the more developed regions generally exhibited little increase in population size and low rates of growth during the period. New York actually had a small population loss between 1970 and 1990, although Los Angeles and Tokyo both registered fairly robust growth for cities in the more developed regions. Two European cities, London and Paris, were respectively the sixth and seventh largest in the world in 1970. By 1990, after a growth rate in the 20-year period of 0.47 per annum, Paris became the fourteenth largest urban agglomeration in the world; London's growth rate during the period was negative (-0.79), and by 1990 it was number 23 in population size among the world urban agglomerations.

TABLE 13.   POPULATION SIZE OF URBAN AGGLOMERATIONS WITH 10 MILLION OR MORE IN 2010, FOR THE YEARS 1970, 1990 AND 2010, AND THEIR AVERAGE ANNUAL RATE OF GROWTH, 1970-1975 AND 2005-2010

Rank in 2010	Agglomeration	Population (millions)			Average annual rate of growth (percentage)	
		1970	1990	2010 [a]	1970-1975	2005-2010 [a]
1	Tokyo, Japan	16.5	25.0	28.7	3.66	0.16
2	Bombay, India	5.8	12.2	24.3	3.31	2.70
3	Shanghai, China	11.2	13.5	21.5	0.51	2.01
4	Lagos, Nigeria	2.0	7.7	20.8	9.77	3.94
5	São Paulo, Brazil	8.1	14.8	20.1	4.08	1.06
6	Jakarta, Indonesia	3.9	9.3	19.2	4.13	2.70
7	Mexico City, Mexico	9.1	15.1	18.2	4.29	0.98
8	Beijing, China	8.1	10.9	17.8	1.10	2.05
9	Karachi, Pakistan	3.1	8.0	17.6	4.89	3.63
10	New York, United States	16.2	16.1	17.3	−0.39	0.39
11	Dhaka, Bangladesh	1.3	5.9	16.0	7.93	4.19
12	Calcutta, India	6.9	10.7	15.6	2.64	2.27
13	Tianjin, China	5.2	9.3	15.6	3.31	2.07
14	Delhi, India	3.5	8.2	15.5	4.52	2.69
15	Los Angeles, United States	8.4	11.5	14.0	1.27	0.49
16	Metro Manila, Philippines	3.5	8.0	13.7	6.93	2.08
17	Cairo, Egypt	5.3	8.6	13.2	2.62	2.06
18	Seoul, Republic of Korea	5.3	10.6	13.0	4.93	0.51
19	Buenos Aires, Argentina	8.4	10.6	12.1	1.64	0.58
20	Istanbul, Turkey	2.8	6.5	11.7	5.12	1.84
21	Rio de Janeiro, Brazil	7.0	9.5	11.1	2.24	0.91
22	Osaka, Japan	9.4	10.5	10.6	0.95	0.00

Source: World Urbanizatioin Prospects: The 1994 Revision (United Nations publication, Sales No. E.95.XIII.12).
    [a]Projected.

79

218.   Table 13 also shows the annual rates of growth for the largest urban agglomerations for two 5-year periods, 1970-1975 and 2005-2010. For most cities, the rate of population increase is expected to decline during 1990-2010, although four of them—Bombay (India), Jakarta (Indonesia), Karachi (Pakistan) and Delhi (India), in addition to Lagos and Dhaka—are still projected to grow in the near future at a rate of more than 3 per cent per annum. All of the fastest-growing largest urban agglomerations, except Lagos, are in Asia.

219.   City size and rates of growth should be examined in the context of a country's urban structure which often reflects the level of development in the country. Generally, the phenomenon described above as "primacy" or the predominance of a single "mega-city" in the hierarchy of urban places is characteristic of less developed regions. In the more developed regions, the pattern is more likely to show a number of large cities, each with a relatively small percentage of the country's total urban population.

220.   Primacy in a country has been associated with the beginning of economic development and modernization, when investment, resources and infrastructure are concentrated in one place to maximize economic efficiency. Employment opportunities in newly established manufacturing industries attract migrants from rural areas. In rapidly growing cities, immigration usually accounts for a larger share of growth than natural increase. As development proceeds, it is expected that its effects will expand to other areas of the country. Employment opportunities and infrastructure will in turn be created in smaller cities and towns, and the primate city will exhibit a declining share of the country's urban population. A more balanced urban structure—one with a network of alternative urban centres with transportation and communication among them—will begin to emerge. The growth of secondary cities often signals the diversification of economic activity and a more equitable distribution of the benefits of development.

221.   In 1990, primacy was apparent in a number of the largest urban agglomerations. Bangkok (Thailand), Lima (Peru) and Buenos Aires (Argentina) all had more than 40 per cent of their country's urban population. Four other cities—Cairo (Egypt), Dhaka (Bangladesh), Seoul (Republic of Korea) and Metro Manila (Philippines)—had more than 30 per cent of the urban population. United Nations projections show that all seven of those urban agglomerations are expected to lose urban share by the year 2010. None will actually lose population—in fact, all but Buenos Aires and Seoul will grow at a rate of more than 2.2 per cent per annum—but growth in other urban areas will outstrip the population increase in those primate cities, leading to a somewhat more balanced distribution of urban population.

222.   Three countries in Asia are exceptions to the general observation about primate cities. China and India, the two most populous countries in the world and both in less developed regions, do not have primate cities, although both are home to some of the largest urban agglomerations in the world. In 1990, 38 cities in China had at least 1 million residents. Its largest urban agglomerations were Shanghai (13.4 million in 1990), Beijing (10.9 million) and Tianjin (9.3 million), but together they constituted only 11.1 per

cent of China's urban population. India, too, has very large urban agglomerations without having primate cities. Bombay, a city of 12.2 million in 1990, along with Calcutta (10.7 million) and Delhi (8.2 million), had 14.4 per cent of India's urban population. This proportion is expected to change slightly by 2010. The third Asian country that does not conform to expectations about primacy is Japan. As a developed country, Japan would be expected to have no dominant primate city; but in 1990 Tokyo had 26.2 per cent of Japan's urban population, up from 22.2 per cent in 1970, and its share is still increasing slowly. By the year 2010 it is expected to be home to just over 28 per cent of Japanese urban-dwellers. The second largest urban agglomeration, Osaka, had 11 per cent of the urban population in 1990.

Policies

223.   The World Population Plan of Action emphasizes, *inter alia*, the need for the integration of population distribution policies with economic and social policies, and urges Governments to promote more equitable regional development, develop a network of small- and medium-sized cities and improve economic and social conditions in rural areas (paras. 44-50). Mexico City recommendations (39-44) further urged Governments to review their socio-economic policies in order to minimize any adverse spatial consequences, improve the integration of population factors in territorial and sectoral planning, implement population distribution policies through incentives, rather than migration control measures, and adopt effective policies to assist women migrants.

224.   Governments throughout the world have adopted and implemented a variety of policies to influence population distribution and internal migration, including incentives and disincentives to influence location decisions of households and firms. In terms of approaches to influencing the spatial distribution of population, Governments continue to pursue, *inter alia*, strategies aimed at countering primacy by promoting growth of small towns and intermediate cities, creation or strengthening of rural growth centres, development of lagging regions, and overall rural development to retain the rural population. In order to implement these population distribution strategies, Governments have taken measures that include subsidies for public infrastructure; grants, loans, or other incentives for relocation of industries and workers; decentralization of administrative, educational and research facilities; and provision of housing and social services on a decentralized basis.

225.   The results of these actions have been mixed, with failures outnumbering success cases. Administrative and legal measures have had only modest impact. For example, although opening new lands for settlements has benefited a small proportion of the rural population, it has not been effective in restraining rural-to-urban migration on a significant scale. Integrated rural development policies, which intended to raise agricultural income and thus persuade people to remain on the farm, have proved overly complex and lacked the necessary resources for effective implementation. In recent years, a number of the costlier population distribution policies, such as relocation of

national capital cities and the establishment of new towns, have been abandoned or curtailed as a result of adverse economic conditions.

226. In order to achieve a balanced spatial distribution of production, employment and population, the Programme of Action recommends that countries should adopt sustainable regional development strategies supported by fiscal decentralization. In addition, it recommends that Governments should provide incentives for the relocation of industries and businesses from urban to rural areas in order to reduce the urban bias and isolated rural development. It also urges countries to increase information and training on conservation practices and to foster the creation of sustainable off-farm rural employment opportunities in order to limit the further expansion of human settlements to areas with fragile ecosystems. Furthermore, it recommends that Governments should enable city and municipal authorities to deal with specific problems such as the management of urban development, the safeguarding of the environment, responding to the needs of all citizens, eliminating health and social problems, and providing individuals with alternatives to living areas prone to natural and man-made disasters. Moreover, the Programme of Action recommends that Governments finance the needed infrastructure and services in the urban environment in a balanced manner and that local and national governmental agencies consider introducing equitable cost-recovery schemes and increasing revenues by appropriate measures. Governments are likewise urged to improve the plight of the urban poor and, in particular, rural migrants and street children. The Programme of Action uses more forceful language than in the past in urging countries to recognize the lands of indigenous people and to protect their communities from activities that are environmentally unsound or are viewed as inappropriate by them. Finally, the Programme of Action urges Governments to recognize and address the needs of internally displaced persons and to find lasting solutions to their plight, including their protection and safe return to their home of origin.

IX. INTERNATIONAL MIGRATION

227. Growing economic interdependence among countries encourages and is, in turn, encouraged by international migration. International migration is a rational response of individuals to the real or perceived economic, social and political differences among countries. Most international migration flows are of a regional nature; however, interregional migration, particularly that directed to the more developed regions, has been growing. It is estimated that there are more than 125 million people outside their country of birth or citizenship in the world and that half of them are from developing countries. A large proportion of the international migrants have migrated voluntarily, but an increasing number are displaced persons and refugees.

228. Table 14 presents the views and policies of Governments in relation to immigration and emigration. In 1993, 2.6 per cent of countries perceived their levels of international immigration as too low; 74.6 per cent perceived their immigration levels as satisfactory; and 22.6 per cent perceived those levels as too high. Among the 190 countries, 4.2 per cent adopted policies to raise their levels, 60.5 per cent desired to maintain their levels, and 35.3 per cent adopted policies to lower their levels.

229. With respect to emigration, in 1993, 3.1 per cent of countries perceived their levels as too low, 75.2 per cent perceived those levels as satisfactory, and 21.7 per cent perceived those levels as too high. In terms of emigration policies, 3.2 per cent of countries sought to raise emigration, 77.4 per cent to maintain current levels, and 19.5 per cent aimed at lowering emigration levels.

230. The World Population Plan of Action recognizes that the significance of international migration varies widely among countries, depending on the area, population size and growth rate, social and economic structure, and environmental conditions. This chapter covers three distinct types of international migrants: documented, undocumented and refugees.

231. The Programme of Action recognizes that orderly international migration can have positive impacts on both the communities of origin and those of destination, but it underscores that the long-term manageability of international migration hinges on making the option to remain in one's country a viable one for all people. To that end, efforts to achieve sustainable economic and social development, and to ensure a better economic balance between developed countries, on the one hand, and developing countries and countries with economies in transition, on the other hand, should be strengthened. However, recognizing that the economic situation of the latter groups of countries is likely to improve only gradually and that, consequently, migration flows originating in them will not decline in the short-to-medium term, Governments are urged to adopt transparent international migration policies and programmes to manage such flows. In particular, Governments are invited to con-

TABLE 14. GOVERNMENTS' PERCEPTIONS AND POLICIES CONCERNING LEVEL
OF IMMIGRATION AND EMIGRATION, 1976-1993
(Percentage of countries)

A. Perceptions

	Immigration				Emigration			
Year	Too low	Satis-factory	Too high	Total	Too low	Satis-factory	Too high	Total
1976	7.1	86.5	6.4	100.0[a]	3.9	83.3	12.8	100.0[c]
1983	6.6	74.4	19.0	100.0[b]	6.0	74.4	19.6	100.0[b]
1986	3.6	76.4	20.0	100.0[c]	5.3	75.3	19.4	100.0[c]
1989	3.5	75.9	20.6	100.0[c]	5.3	74.1	20.6	100.0[c]
1993	2.6	74.6	22.6	100.0[d]	3.1	75.2	21.7	100.0[d]

B. Policies

	Immigration				Emigration			
Year	To raise	To maintain[c]	To lower	Total	To raise	To maintain[c]	To lower	Total
1976	7.1	86.5	6.4	100.0[a]	3.8	83.4	12.8	100.0[a]
1983	4.0	77.9	16.7	100.0[b]	4.8	75.0	20.2	100.0[b]
1986	3.5	77.1	19.4	100.0[c]	4.7	73.5	21.8	100.0[c]
1989	4.7	63.7	31.8	100.0[c]	3.5	71.8	24.7	100.0[c]
1993	4.2	60.5	35.3	100.0[d]	3.2	77.4	19.5	100.0[d]

Source: Population Policy Data Bank maintained by the Population Division of the Department for Economic and Social Information and Policy Analysis of the United Nations Secretariat.

[a]Representing 156 countries.
[b]Representing 168 countries.
[c]Representing 170 countries.
[d]Representing 190 countries.
[e]Also including those countries that decided not to intervene.

sider the use of temporary migration as a means of improving the skills of nationals of developing countries and those with economies in transition.

Issue No. 18. Documented migrants

Trends

232. Trends in documented migration at the global level remain difficult to assess because many countries known to receive significant numbers of legal migrants either lack adequate flow statistics or fail to disseminate them. In addition, the lack of comparability of available statistics severely limits the inferences that can be made from them. Thus, although there is some evidence suggesting that legal migration to the industrialized Western bloc countries increased between the early and the late 1980s, this assertion must be qualified. The countries of permanent immigration, for instance, admitted about 4 million immigrants during 1980-1984 and some 4.5 million in 1985-1989, with these numbers excluding the 100,000 or so persons admitted annually as temporary migrants and the nearly 3 million undocumented migrants whose status was regularized by United States authorities in the late 1980s and early 1990s. In comparison, the main receiving countries of North-

ern and Western Europe recorded about 4.6 million incoming migrants during 1980-1984 and 6.3 million during 1985-1989. However, most of those migrants were not admitted on a long-term basis. Indeed, when emigration is taken into account, the main receiving countries in Europe registered net migration losses during 1980-1984 followed by a net migration gain of over 2 million persons during 1985-1989. The increased emigration of ethnic Germans from Eastern Europe to the former Federal Republic of Germany, where they had the right to citizenship, accounted for a major portion of that gain; more generally, the relaxation of exit restrictions resulting from the changes taking place in Eastern Europe and the former USSR during the 1980s was largely responsible for the increases in net migration to Western European countries during that decade.

233. The oil-producing countries of Western Asia constituted another important focus of attraction for documented migrants during the 1980s, although their importance declined somewhat during the decade, as falling oil prices slowed their economic growth and their labour-force needs fell. Although there are no adequate statistics on the number of migrant workers admitted by those countries, data gathered by the main sending countries indicate that the outflow of temporary workers from the latter averaged about 1 million persons per annum during the 1980s and that, towards the end of the decade, increasing proportions of workers headed towards destinations other than those in Western Asia. In particular, Japan and the newly industrializing economies of Eastern and South-eastern Asia began attracting foreign workers towards the end of the 1980s, as their local labour markets became increasingly tight. During the early 1990s, the Gulf crisis forced the repatriation of some 700,000 foreign workers from Western Asia, but once it was over, migration to the region seems to have resumed.

Policies

234. The Plan of Action addresses the needs of documented migrants by focusing mostly on those admitted as workers. Thus, it instructs Governments of receiving countries to provide proper treatment and adequate welfare services to migrant workers and their families (para. 55) and to prevent discrimination against them in the labour market and in society, to preserve their human rights, to combat prejudice against them and to eliminate obstacles to the reunion of their families (para. 56). The International Conference on Population reiterated this appeal (Mexico City recommendations 48 and 49) and invited Governments to use relevant ILO conventions as guidelines in achieving their aim (recommendation 48). Progress in the implementation of those recommendations has been slow. In the main receiving countries, few measures have been taken to improve the rights or the situation of documented migrant workers during the past decade. In Europe, the high unemployment rates recorded in a number of countries during the late 1980s and early 1990s fuelled anti-immigrant feelings and led to more restrictive migration policies, especially in relation to family reunification. In most of the receiving countries of Western Asia, migrant workers are still far from enjoying equality of opportunity and treatment with nationals in terms of working conditions; and the lack of effective protection of the basic rights of female

migrant workers remains a cause for concern. Furthermore, the Gulf crisis, by forcing the repatriation of large numbers of migrant workers, accentuated their vulnerability.

235. Advances in the implementation of international instruments related to migrant workers have also been modest. Thus, between 1982 and 1991, three States ratified the ILO Convention concerning Migration for Employment (No. 97) and another three acceded to the ILO Convention concerning Migrations in Abusive Conditions and the Promotion of Equality of Opportunity and Treatment of Migrant Workers (No. 143), bringing to 38 and 15, respectively, the total number of States parties to such Conventions.[1] Consequently, although the adoption in 1990 by the General Assembly (resolution 45/158) of the International Convention on the Protection of the Rights of All Migrant Workers and Members of Their Families represented a major step towards ensuring the international protection of migrant workers, its ratification is expected to proceed slowly. By the end of 1993, only Mexico and Morocco had signed the Convention. Ratification by 20 States is needed for the Convention to enter into force. The Convention sets forth the basic principles concerning the treatment of migrant workers and members of their families and distinguishes the rights that are to be accorded to all migrant workers, irrespective of the regularity of their status in the receiving State, from those that apply only to migrant workers in a regular situation (part IV of the Convention). It thus establishes standards for the treatment of both documented and undocumented migrants.

236. Both the Plan of Action (paras. 57 and 58) and Mexico City recommendation 46 address the issue of the outflow of skilled workers from developing countries and suggest, among other things, that the Governments of countries of origin expand employment opportunities to retain those workers. Although data on the migration of skilled personnel are far from ideal, the evidence suggests that during the 1980s developing countries themselves were increasingly the destination of skilled migrants originating in both other developing countries and the developed world. Some programmes, such as that instituted in 1974 by the International Organization for Migration (IOM), have assisted skilled workers to return to their countries of origin. Thus, since 1974, 13,000 professional, technical and kindred workers have returned to Latin America with IOM assistance, and almost 600 returned to Africa during 1983-1988. In the United Nations system, experts assigned to developing countries with skill shortages are increasingly recruited from developing countries. However, most skilled personnel migrate in response to market forces and their convergence on certain developing countries results from the favourable opportunities that they offer. Persons with needed skills are expected to be in high demand, both in the developed and in the most economically dynamic developing countries. It is noteworthy that in amending their immigration laws in 1990, both Japan and the United States accorded higher priority to the admission of skilled migrants.

237. The Plan of Action calls for developed countries to cooperate with developing countries to create more favourable employment opportunities in countries of origin through the increased availability of capital, technical assistance, export markets and more favourable terms of trade (para. 54). Im-

proving the access to export markets of the products of developing countries was the subject of negotiations in the context of the multilateral trade liberalization negotiations, known as the Uruguay Round, which was successfully concluded in early 1994. While freer trade is not expected to replace international migration, it is generally acknowledged that in the long run, trade liberalization will foster development and thus eventually reduce pressures to migrate from the developing countries.

238. With respect to documented migrants, the Programme of Action recommends that Governments consider facilitating the naturalization of those having the right to long-term residence. It further stresses the need to enhance the integration of the children of long-term documented migrants by providing them with educational and training opportunities equal to those of nationals and allowing them to exercise an economic activity. Of special importance is that Governments promote the integration of family reunification provisions in their national legislation in a manner consistent with article 10 of the Convention on the Rights of the Child.

Issue No. 19. Undocumented migrants

Trends

239. Considering that the main receiving countries are increasingly restricting the admission of documented migrants, undocumented migration is probably on the rise, though by its very nature it is difficult to quantify. During the 1980s, the United States was the country hosting the largest undocumented population in the world, amounting to several million persons. In addition, the former labour-sending countries of southern Europe began to attract migrants, most of whom had little choice but to be undocumented, given the lack of provisions for their legal admission. Towards the end of the 1980s, Japan also emerged as an important destination of irregular migration and so did some of the newly industrializing countries of Eastern and South-eastern Asia. In fact, migration between developing countries has often been of an irregular nature, since receiving countries generally lack both the provisions and the enforcement mechanisms to control international migration.

Policies

240. Both the Plan of Action (para. 56) and Mexico City recommendations 52 and 53 urge Governments to respect the basic human rights of undocumented migrants, to prevent their exploitation and to combat the activities of those inducing or facilitating undocumented migration. As noted above, the International Convention on the Protection of the Rights of All Migrant Workers and Members of Their Families has established international standards regarding the rights of undocumented migrant workers. The Convention grants those migrants and members of their families equality of treatment with nationals with regard to remuneration and conditions of work, social security, and access to urgent medical care and education. The Convention also urges Governments to impose sanctions on the employers of undocumented migrants and on those who organize irregular migration. It further provides

guidelines for Governments that wish to regularize the status of undocumented migrants.

241. During the 1980s a number of countries adopted measures to control undocumented migration. In 1986, the United States adopted the Immigration Reform and Control Act (IRCA) which established provisions for the eventual regularization of nearly 3 million undocumented migrants and imposed sanctions on employers who knowingly hired undocumented migrants. IRCA allowed for the regularization of two groups of undocumented migrants: illegal aliens who had been in the United States since before 1 January 1982, and those who had been employed in seasonal agricultural work for at least 90 days during the year ending on 1 May 1986. By the end of 1991, 2.5 million undocumented migrants had been granted permanent residence status under the provisions of IRCA. The success of employer sanctions in curbing the inflow of undocumented migrants to the United States has been mixed, in part because of their weak enforcement.

242. In the late 1980s, Italy and Spain also undertook regularization drives for undocumented aliens as part of the process of framing new immigration laws. In Italy, about 105,000 aliens qualified for legalization during 1987-1988 and another 216,000 in 1990, while in Spain, a total of 177,000 undocumented migrants applied for legalization under campaigns carried out in the period 1985-1986 and 1991.

243. In the European Community, the drive to create a single market and eliminate internal border controls has triggered a range of measures aimed at controlling undocumented migration into Community territory. Apart from increasing the surveillance of their external borders, countries that signed the Convention on the Application of the Schengen Agreement concluded a readmission agreement with Poland, by which Poland agreed to take back undocumented Polish migrants. In addition, in 1991 member States of the European Community agreed on a list of countries whose nationals needed visas to enter Community territory. Increasingly, the adoption of visa requirements, the imposition of fines on airlines that carry passengers without valid documents and the outright deportation of undocumented migrants have been used as measures to curb irregular migration throughout Europe. In addition, countries such as France and the Netherlands have increased the penalties imposed on employers of undocumented migrants, and Germany has adopted a series of measures facilitating the control of migrant workers.

244. Regarding undocumented migration, Governments of countries of origin and those of destination are urged to cooperate in reducing its causes and safeguarding the basic human rights of undocumented migrants, including their right to seek and enjoy asylum from persecution. The adoption of effective sanctions against those who organize undocumented migration, exploit undocumented migrants or engage in trafficking of undocumented migrants is strongly recommended, particularly when the migrants involved are women, young persons or children. The responsibility that Governments of countries of origin have to accept the return and reintegration of undocumented migrants and asylum-seekers and to avoid penalizing such persons on their return is underscored.

245.   Refugee movements are a facet of broader migratory movements. While there might be a number of contributory factors to refugee outflows, their specificity derives from the determination of what constitutes a refugee. The Statute of the Office of the United Nations High Commissioner for Refugees (UNHCR) identifies as refugees those persons who flee their country or stay away from it because of a well-founded fear of persecution for reasons of race, religion, nationality or political opinion.[2] A similar definition is found in the Convention relating to the Status of Refugees and its 1967 Protocol, the latter containing in its definition membership in a particular social group as a ground for fear of persecution. Somewhat refined definitions are found in the 1969 Organization of African Unity (OAU) Convention[3] and in the 1984 Cartagena Declaration on Refugees, adopted by the Colloquium on the International Protection of Refugees in Central America, Panama and Mexico; both documents take into account refugee-generating factors such as external aggression, occupation, foreign domination or events seriously disturbing public order, internal conflicts, and the massive violation of human rights. These two regional definitions refer in fact to categories of persons to whom UNHCR has extended protection and assistance since the late 1950s. On the basis of these legal instruments and the Cartagena Declaration, a broad spectrum of causes have been identified that allow for the recognition of refugee-type movements within the wider phenomenon of migratory movements.

246.   Currently, the international community is confronted with humanitarian emergencies on a hitherto unknown scale. It is becoming ever more important to understand the underlying political, social, economic, demographic and environmental reasons that compel people to move. It is only through a better appreciation of the complexity and interrelatedness of the causes of displacement that a comprehensive approach to the refugee issue will be found.

Trends

247.   According to UNHCR sources, early in 1993 there were nearly 19 million refugees[4] and by 1994 the total population of concern to the High Commissioner for Refugees had reached 23 million, of which 16.4 million were refugees and the rest were persons in need of protection who did not have refugee status. In addition, there were 2.5 million Palestinian refugees under the mandate of the United Nations Relief and Works Agency for Palestine Refugees in the Near East (UNRWA). Between 1984 and 1991, the number of refugees in the world had doubled, passing from 8 million to 16 million. During most of the 1980s and up to 1994, most refugees were in the developing world. In 1993, nearly 9 out of every 10 refugees had found asylum in developing countries, some of which are among the poorest in the world. No region in the world is spared the impact of the tragic and increasingly complex refugee phenomenon, and the presence of refugees has imposed considerable strains on the meagre resources of certain countries, particularly those in Africa. Developed countries have also had difficulties in coping with the growing numbers of asylum-seekers whose cases sometimes

take years to be adjudicated and who often do not qualify for refugee status. In response to such developments, a number of developed countries have adopted measures to streamline their asylum adjudication procedures and to control the admission of would-be asylum-seekers so as to prevent the abuse of the asylum system.

248. A significant number of refugees in the world are women. UNHCR estimated that in 1993, 48 per cent of all refugees were women and that, in Africa, women constituted 50.5 per cent of the refugee population. Together with children, women account therefore for a major proportion of the world's refugees. Because the specific needs of women and children have important programmatic implications for UNHCR activities in the areas of international protection and assistance, the Executive Committee of UNHCR has highlighted the importance of comprehensive refugee statistics by sex, especially to plan gender-sensitive programmes. Furthermore, in October 1992, the Executive Committee called on the High Commissioner for Refugees to pursue her efforts to increase public awareness of the rights and protection needs of two potentially vulnerable groups—namely, refugee women, and girls (United Nations, 1993f). In regard to the protection and well-being of refugee children, the Executive Committee emphasized the particular situation of unaccompanied minors.

249. Large numbers of refugees in the world are still to be found in the least developed countries. The problem of refugees and that of their impact on national socio-economic infrastructures and the development process itself cannot be treated in isolation from each other. Likewise, the socio-economic situation prevailing in the refugee's country of origin cannot be disregarded in any comprehensive analysis of contributory factors to the root causes of refugee outflows.

Policies

250. The General Assembly, in its resolution 47/105 re-emphasized the need to keep issues relating to refugees, displaced persons, asylum-seekers and other migratory flows firmly in the international political agenda, especially the question of solution-oriented approaches to deal with such contemporary problems and their causes. Nobody can ignore the socio-economic factors that contribute to displacement or hinder the attainment of durable solutions. It is felt that the deepening global economic crisis, greater environmental degradation, the heavier debt burden, conditions of absolute poverty, and the failure of the international community to develop a strategy to address those issues could most likely aggravate the refugee problem.

251. Mexico City recommendation 54 urges Governments to accede to the 1951 Convention relating to the Status of Refugees and its 1967 Protocol, which constitute the basis for the international asylum system. Progress has been substantial, with over 20 States having acceded to the instruments during 1982-1992. As of August 1992, 111 States were parties to either the 1951 Convention or the 1967 Protocol.

252. Mexico City recommendation 55 also urges Governments and international organizations to find durable solutions to the problems related to

refugees, particularly by providing assistance to first-asylum countries, creating conditions conducive to the voluntary repatriation of refugees, and facilitating the local integration of those refugees for whom resettlement or repatriation is not possible.

253. With the easing of international tensions, there are, of late, increased opportunities for voluntary repatriation. Such return movements need to be completed by development initiatives, since the country of intended return is frequently one affected by extreme poverty and having virtually no productive capacity and very limited basic facilities and infrastructure. The significant contribution that development assistance can make towards the preferred solution of voluntary repatriation[5] needs to be emphasized. UNHCR has been making particular efforts to involve development agencies in voluntary repatriation drives, hoping thereby to assure the durable nature of voluntary repatriation movements.

254. The changes that have taken place since the end of the cold war have had important implications for the international refugee regime. Such changes have created a new spirit of international cooperation favourable to the resolution of the regional and internal conflicts that were at the root of many of the world refugee problems. With many conflicts thus resolved, some 2 million refugees were able to return home in 1992 alone. In fact, during the late 1980s, a number of successful repatriation drives were carried out in the developing countries, particularly in Africa, where they involved, among others, Ethiopian, Namibian and Ugandan refugees. The conflict in Mozambique was one of those whose resolution owed much to the end of the cold war. Thus, the peace agreement, concluded in 1992 between the warring parties, raised hopes for the eventual repatriation of nearly 1 million refugees. Similarly, the process of normalization of political life that is taking place in Cambodia and that started in October 1991 when the four warring factions signed agreements on a comprehensive political settlement (the Paris Agreements) has allowed the repatriation of over 300,000 displaced Cambodians. In Central America, the peace process made possible by the reduction of super-Power rivalry has led to a significant reduction in the refugee and displaced population in the region. However, in several cases the resolution of conflict has failed to materialize. Thus, although the 1988 Geneva accords (Agreements on the Settlement of the Situation Relating to Afghanistan) raised prospects for the repatriation of the more than 5.5 million Afghan refugees in the Islamic Republic of Iran and Pakistan, civil war prevented their return. In 1992, however, over half a million Afghan refugees opted for repatriation. Also elusive was the resolution of conflict in Angola, where the hope of repatriation has largely vanished.

255. A major change occurring during the 1980s was the increase in the number of persons seeking asylum directly in the developed countries. Until the early 1980s, most of the refugees admitted by those countries had been resettled from countries of first asylum and could therefore be screened abroad. In many of the receiving countries, the need to examine asylum claims on a case-by-case basis soon led to considerable backlogs. The practice of granting work permits to asylum-seekers while they awaited the result of the adjudication procedure provided an incentive for abuse of the system. These de-

velopments have led developed countries, particularly those in Europe and Northern America, to adopt measures that both control the growth of asylum claims and prevent abuse. Thus, in June 1990, member States of the European Community adopted the Dublin Convention which determined which State would be responsible for adjudicating an asylum request, thus preventing the making of simultaneous claims in several States. In addition, a variety of measures have been taken by European and Northern American countries to remove manifestly unfounded claims at an early stage of the asylum procedure and even to prevent claims from being filed altogether. The use of the "safe country" principle, for instance, prevents citizens of countries deemed safe from applying for asylum. Germany, one of the major destinations of asylum-seekers, changed its constitution in 1993 so as to be able to apply such a principle.

256.   Such developments, together with those mentioned above in connection with the control of undocumented migration (the imposition of visa requirements or of fines on airlines transporting passengers without proper documentation), have effectively increased the barriers to international population movement and as a result are likely to prevent not only the entry of undocumented migrants but also that of bona fide refugees in need of protection. In particular, the safe-country principle established by the 1951 Convention may infringe the individual's right to seek asylum, and the practice of sending back migrants without proper documentation may be inconsistent with the principle of *non-refoulement*, which prevents the forcible return of persons fearing persecution to places where their lives or freedom may be threatened.

257.   Often, persons seeking asylum are not fleeing individual persecution but rather generalized violence, ethnic conflict or civil war. Refugee movements are thus more than a serious humanitarian and human rights issue; often they reflect destabilizing situations that affect international security. Indeed, in areas that were previously under strong super-Power influence, there has been a recrudescence of nationalist sentiments and ethnic tensions that have led to conflict and population displacement. Furthermore, there is a growing appreciation of other contributory factors to migratory and refugee movements—namely, developmental and environmental considerations, and a greater sensitivity to the demographic make-up of refugee populations. Whereas in the past, individuals fleeing communist regimes were automatically considered refugees by Western bloc countries and were generally granted permanent settlement rights because they were deemed unlikely to return to their countries of origin, in the 1990s more people are being granted only temporary protection while the situation that gave rise to their flight subsides. Furthermore, new modes of protection are emerging. Thus, the end of super-Power rivalry has allowed the international community to intervene on behalf of internally displaced persons. The creation of safe havens for the Kurdish population within northern Iraq in 1991 and of protected areas in Croatia in 1992 provides a salient example of this trend.

258.   The United Nations Conference on Environment and Development provided UNHCR with the opportunity to reflect on the relationship between environmental degradation and population movements. Environmental

degradation can itself be a contributory factor to refugee flows. In cases where environmental changes are a consequence of or lead to the violation of basic human rights, there might be a valid claim for international protection on the part of those who flee. In addition, environmental considerations can and do influence the asylum policies of receiving countries, particularly when large numbers of refugees arrive in ecologically fragile areas.

259.   UNHCR is now emphasizing the pursuit, where possible, of a strategy involving preventive activities, including the protection of displaced persons in their country of origin. Such an endeavour could be described as comprising efforts to attenuate or avert refugee flows. While prevention is a promising strategy, it has its limits and is not a substitute for asylum.

260.   Recognizing the growing complexity of the factors leading to refugee flows and population displacement, the Programme of Action urges Governments to address the root causes of such movements by, among other things, engaging in conflict resolution, promoting peace and the respect of human rights, and respecting the sovereignty of States. Governments are encouraged to enhance regional and international mechanisms that promote appropriate shared responsibility for the protection and assistance of refugees. More specifically, adequate international support should be extended to countries of asylum so that they can meet the basic needs of refugees. The need to create conditions that allow the voluntary repatriation of refugees in safety and dignity is stressed, noting that rehabilitation assistance to repatriating refugees should be linked to long-term reconstruction and development plans. The principle of *non-refoulement* is reiterated, and Governments are urged to consider granting at least temporary protection to refugees and displaced persons arriving suddenly and in large numbers. The need to devise special protection measures for refugee women and children is underscored.

NOTES

[1] Unlike the World Population Plan of Action or the recommendations, resolutions and decisions adopted by the International Conference on Population (Mexico City, 1984), the ILO conventions are international legal instruments that enter into force and become binding upon ratification by the States parties to such conventions. In effect, they become part of the States' laws and thus overrule any independent international committee of experts.

[2] See General Assembly resolution 428 (V) of 14 December 1950, annex, para. 6 (A) (ii).

[3] See OAU Convention Governing the Specific Aspects of Refugee Problems in Africa, 1969 (1001 UNTS 45).

[4] Refugee statistics available to UNHCR as at 30 June 1992. The Executive Committee of the Office of the United Nations High Commissioner for Refugees recently stated (A/AC.96/804, para. 32 (r)) that it recognized the difficulties associated with the compilation of refugee statistics but, given the importance of such statistics, especially for gender-sensitive programme planning, urged UNHCR to pursue proposals set out by the committee.

[5] General Assembly resolution 47/105, para. 9.

X. POPULATION INFORMATION, EDUCATION
AND COMMUNICATION

261.   Since the adoption of the World Population Plan of Action in 1974, there have been important efforts to promote awareness and understanding of population issues among Governments, non-governmental organizations, communities, families and individuals. Such efforts have also aimed at mobilizing the support of national administrators, decision makers and opinion leaders in favour of population policies and programmes. The basic goal has been to provide access to clear and accurate population information. Although it is difficult to measure the impact of such efforts on different audiences, it has been widely accepted that activities of this type drive policies and programmes, and individual and community behaviour.

262.   The term "information, education and communication" alludes to a large variety of activities usually having a broad mandate and complex functions and involving many different audiences, messages and channels of communication. Nevertheless, it is normally used to refer to the fostering of interest in a particular subject. In the area of, say, family planning, the term could allude to a series of specific goals, such as creating public awareness about the need for family planning; increasing knowledge about the use and risks of family-planning methods, or about where to obtain contraceptives; and motivating couples and individuals to visit family-planning services.

263.   When specific target audiences are identified, it is expected that information, education and communication will produce a kind of behavioural modification in the intended group, as is the case in the promotion of "safe sex" for the prevention of AIDS. In the field of population, in general, target audiences are more and more concentrated at the grass-roots level.

264.   Nevertheless, the term "information, education and communication" has some unclear connotations. For example, it could be used as an umbrella term to refer to technical information, which is different in its content and goals from information aimed at motivating certain types of behaviour. This chapter takes into account these two broad types of information and concentrates on two particular issues—namely, the accurate and objective information that is needed for policy-making and programme management, and the information that is aimed at increasing the level of awareness about population issues.

Issue No. 21.   Technical information

265.   The term "technical information" includes basic data, collected using reliable scientific methods such as censuses and surveys, and the findings and implications of objective research studies. Accurate up-to-date technical information is needed by policy makers and programme managers for

the formulation of policies and programme goals and for the preparation of the operational plans needed to achieve those goals. Technical population information constitutes the knowledge base upon which to build sound population policies and programmes. Such information is found in a variety of printed and electronic forms. Users of this type of information may address their requests to national statistical offices, population research institutes and universities, but more and more, they are directing their requests to population information centres that have been specifically set up for this purpose.

266. Many countries lack adequate resources and institutional mechanisms for the collection, storage and processing of their population data. Shortages of trained manpower, the lack of appropriate technology and inadequate financial resources also contribute to the absence of national information infrastructures, particularly in the developing countries. As indicated in Agenda 21, even where information is available, it may not be easily accessible either because of a lack of technology for effective access or because of associated costs, especially for information held outside the country and available commercially (United Nations, 1993b).

267. Population information centres have three main functions: to identify, collect, organize and store population-related information; to analyse, synthesize, tailor and repackage the data and information to suit the needs of the various types of users they serve; and to retrieve and disseminate the information in both its original and its repackaged formats. The information that is needed for the monitoring and evaluation of programme performance is generally gathered through management information systems that have been established for that purpose.

268. The Plan of Action includes various recommendations on the dissemination of information and research results (paras. 88, 91 and 92), which were echoed in Mexico City recommendation 76. Concerning the dissemination and exchange of technical information, it is important to mention that the field of population has been well served through an array of serial publications that have a long tradition of high standards. The English-language journals *Demography, Population and Development Review* and *Population Studies* and the French-language journal *Population* are well known among scholars and constitute an additional source of technical information beyond the technical publications of the United Nations, which include the *Population Bulletin of the United Nations*, the *Demographic Yearbook* and the periodical publications of the regional commissions.[1]

269. One of the most significant recent developments is the spread of national, regional and international information databases and networks. A notable example is the global Population Information Network (POPIN). (In its resolution 1979/33, the Economic and Social Council requested the Secretary-General, *inter alia*, to facilitate the establisliment of POPIN.) A decentralized network for the coordination of population information activities in the various regions and the facilitation of worldwide access to population information, POPIN links more than 100 libraries, clearing-houses and documentation and information centres for the purpose of improving the dissemination of population information. There are regional POPINs in Africa (POPIN-

AFRICA), Asia and the Pacific (ASIA-PACIFIC POPIN) and Latin America and the Caribbean (Information Network on Population for Latin America and the Caribbean (IPALCA)). The availability of population information and literature has also been enhanced through the use of electronic resources such as the POPIN Gopher and by the establishinent of computerized international, regional and national bibliographic databases, such as POPLINE, maintained by the Population Information Programme of Johns Hopkins University and Princeton University; DOCPAL, maintained by the Latin American Demographic Centre/Economic Commission for Latin America and the Caribbean (CELADE/ECLAC), Santiago, Chile; the Population File of ESCAP Bibliographic Information System (EBIS POPFILE), maintained by the Economic and Social Commission for Asia and the Pacific (ESCAP), Bangkok; POPINDEX-Africa, maintained by POPIN-AFRICA/Ecónomic Commission for Africa (ECA), Addis Ababa; DOCPOP, maintained by the Fundação Sistema Estadual de Análise de Dados (SEADE), São Paulo, Brazil; and RESADOC, maintained by the Sahel Institute, Bamako.

270.   In order to promote both effective and equitable access to population information, the United Nations system should encourage and facilitate initiatives to strengthen national information capabilities and, whenever possible, should promote the establisliment and use of electronic links for sharing information, providing access to databases and other sources of information, facilitating national and international communication, and transferring data.

Issue No. 22.   Creating awareness

271.   Through various means and channels—including population education in schools, non-formal educational programmes serving people of different ages, extension programmes in health, nutrition and agriculture, and the broad utilization of traditional media—population-related knowledge and motivation have been provided; this has fostered interest, created demand and otherwise supported population programme activities. Experience gained in the implementation of population education and information activities in the past 20 years suggests three important criteria to be taken into account:

(*a*)   Use of the most modern media available for maximum effectiveness;

(*b*)   Use of multimedia that tries to reach a maximum coverage; and

(*c*)   Use of traditional media and local entertainment events in order to reach grass-roots communities and the illiterate audience.

Population education

272.   Mass media can play an important role in raising awareness of population issues, the importance of family planning and the location of services and in establishing a positive atmosphere for national population programmes and family-planning activities. Nevertheless, it has been increasingly recognized that attitudes that form the basis for behaviour and views on population issues are often formed early in life. For this reason, an approach

beginning long before adulthood, such as population education in the school system, is required. Secondary education should reinforce the learning promoted through primary education and should take into account the specific needs of the school-age population. Population education may take place in many settings. It may begin with educational activities for newlywed couples, followed by parent education to help partners educate their own children, and the cycle might continue with the education of children in schools.

273.   During the past decade, the number of countries offering national population education activities in their formal and non-formal education systems increased considerably. At present, population education programmes are found in over 80 countries in the developing world. Their aims vary from country to country, but they are generally designed to introduce understanding and a sense of responsibility regarding population issues. An increase of 54 per cent was registered in the number of countries that had population education programmes carried out in collaboration with UNESCO and UNFPA, notably in Africa. Over the past two decades, important efforts have been made to develop and improve the contents and messages to be incorporated in national population education programmes. The conceptual and methodological approaches, comparative analytical studies and prototype teaching/learning materials produced have made important contributions to the advancement of population education. The provision of technical assistance services has included training workshops and awareness and orientation programmes for educators.

274.   In spite of such progress, most national population education programmes have been constrained by limited political support and commitment at various levels; absence of a firm policy and its implementation on a continuing basis; limited availability of national data and relevant social research findings on the effects of socio-cultural factors on demographic change; shortage of resource materials and teaching staff adequately trained in all aspects of population dynamics; and limited financial support from national and international agencies. These have reduced their effectiveness, threatened their continuity and delayed their expansion.

275.   Considering that the majority of the population in the developing countries is rural and that the demographic behaviour of rural/agricultural households includes specific traits that ought to be carefully considered when designing population IEC activities, a specific area under development at FAO is population education in agricultural extension. Target groups for such activities are agricultural education and extension staff (trainers and subject-matter specialists, trainees and in-service extension workers) and farming families, with particular attention to their youth. Population education topics concretely related to agricultural production, farm management, sustainable agricultural development and environment have been integrated into agricultural extension curricula in selected countries. Methodological adaptation, material production and dissemination effort will continue in this area at least until 1995.

276.   Another area of activity has been the design and production of materials and the training of trainers in the context of informal education programmes for out-of-school rural youth. Booklets have been developed to dis-

seminate knowledge and generate discussions at the community level on human reproduction, family life, population and agriculture, natural resources and the environment. FAO has conducted fieldwork to test the material in selected countries of Africa and Asia, with the cooperation of local associations of rural youth and young farmers. This line of activity is also expanding to all the developing regions.

277. Population education is also part of women-in-development programmes. The target group is rural women of child-bearing age who are beneficiaries of agricultural development programmes and projects. FAO has conducted a series of baseline studies on the linkages between rural women's productive and reproductive roles and the effects of such linkages on family size and structure and on agricultural production and rural development. Results have been instrumental in the preparation of outline formats for non-formal population education activities addressed to rural women.

278. FAO has also been innovative regarding the introduction of population education elements into programmes and curricula geared to nutrition education (an area that has been steadily developing since the late 1970s for the benefit of field programme staff and formal training institutions). Pedagogic supplements on relevant population factors and their relationship with nutrition factors have been developed, tested, translated, adapted and widely applied.

279. With the emergence of AIDS and its socio-demographic consequences, the need for preventive education has acquired a new dimension. As a follow-up to the UNESCO International Conference on Education, convened in Geneva in 1986, teaching materials have been prepared which take into account the socio-cultural aspects of AIDS transmission; awareness and orientation seminars have been organized; and pilot activities have been launched within the framework of population education programmes at the regional level. At the country level, most programmes have introduced elements of AIDS prevention under the sex and family component of population education.

280. UNESCO and UNFPA jointly organized the First International Congress on Population Education and Development, held in Istanbul, Turkey, in April 1993. In preparation for the Congress, UNESCO organized five regional meetings, in 1990 and 1991, with the participation of more than 130 specialists from 85 countries and international organizations. The Congress, which was attended by representatives of 91 Governments (including 20 ministers), underlined the strong global support for population education in school systems. It adopted the Istanbul Declaration on the Role of Population Education in and Its Contribution to the Promotion of Human Development. The Congress also adopted the Action Framework for Population Education on the Eve of the Twenty-first Century, intended as a reference and a guide for Governments, international organizations, bilateral aid agencies and non-governmental organizations when formulating their plans to implement the Istanbul Declaration.

281. In order to meet the challenges of training the younger generations of administrators, decision makers, policy makers and teachers of the

twenty-first century who are currently students in various universities and institutions of higher education in all parts of the world, and as a follow-up to the Congress, which stressed the need for the extension of population education to all educational levels, including that of higher education, efforts need to be made to promote the teaching of population education at the university level. Inter-university cooperation in the field of population education between countries could be established through university twinning and other linking arrangements in connection with the UNESCO Twinning Arrangements (UNITWIN) project and through the establishment of UNESCO chairs in population education and sustainable development.

282. Population education is a rapidly developing field that is already consolidating its approaches and methods. There are, however, new challenges to be met in its conceptualization and institutionalization and in the expansion of population education to encompass all levels of formal and non-formal education in all countries. Like any other subject, population education needs to adapt itself to changing needs and situations. In view of the expanded vision of the role of education, as advocated in the 1990 World Conference on Education for All, held in Jomtien, Thailand, and in the Rio Declaration on Environment and Development (United Nations, 1993b), adopted at the United Nations Conference on Environment and Development, it has become more important than ever to broaden the scope of population education to address in an integrated way the issues of population, development, the environment and gender relations. Various other needs, such as the training of teaching staff, coordination among different educational institutions, knowledge gaps to be filled, sensitization of policy makers, production of a variety of teaching materials, and timely evaluation of related activities should be emphasized.

283. As a new approach, the Programme of Action sets an overall time-bound goal of 2015 as the year by which all countries should make primary education available to all boys and girls. Beyond universal access to primary education, it urges countries to promote secondary and higher education. It also recommends that attention be given to the quality and type of education provided, including a recognition of traditional values. In addition, it urges countries to take affirmative steps to encourage girls to stay in school by, *inter alia*, sensitizing parents and teachers to the value of educating them.

Population communication

284. During the past two decades the world has experienced a significant revolution in the field of communications, which has been stimulated by rapid urbanization (which creates ever larger audiences with wider access to mass media); large numbers of young people who are more closely attuned to the impact of mass media; increasing access to audio-visual communication techniques and widespread use of radios, televisions and video cassette recorders;[2] and the development of new technologies for storing and processing information (for example, compact discs, easy-to-use data transmission, microcomputers and software). Such developments have reached a large range of audiences (including those at the local grass-roots level) and have been ac-

companied by the recognition of the need to improve the quality of communication between providers of services and their clients.

285. Special efforts have been made to organize population training workshops and courses for professional communicators who work in development programmes. These training programmes provide both communication skills and knowledge for the application of information technologies to addressing population issues and strengthening the management of population communication programmes.

286. A large number of projects have provided technical assistance, training and equipment for the production and distribution of population communication materials aimed at establishing links with regional media networks and national broadcasting institutions in order to promote population issues in their programming. In line with priority activities to enhance the status of women in society, a number of projects were launched by UNESCO in cooperation with national radio and television stations, including the production of television spots and drama on topics related to improving the status of women through education, family planning, changing gender roles and marriage counselling. Note should be taken of the importance of such activities in conveying appropriate messages effectively to target audiences.

287. UNESCO has a joint project with UNEP called the International Environmental Education Programme (IEEP). This project and the UNFPA/UNESCO action scheme on population information, education and communication are two key mechanisms for inter-agency cooperation. A new UNESCO interdisciplinary and inter-agency cooperation project, Environment and Population Education and Information for Development, which was approved by UNESCO's General Conference at its twenty-seventh session in November 1993, aims at the development of education, training and information activities designed to deal with the interwoven issues of population, environment and human development, including gender perspectives, in an integrated, manner, with emphasis on specific and problem-solving research and action.

288. Population communication efforts for rural populations have undergone continuous development. The emphasis has been on developing methods to address illiterate populations at the community grass-roots level. Rural radio has been used in many contexts. Community-participative approaches to identifying topics for communication programmes (and select visual aids) on the basis of socio-cultural research have been used extensively. FAO has reviewed its own development support communication programmes so as to introduce population-related topics, where applicable.

289. FAO has designed programmes aimed at improving the capabilities of agricultural policy makers and programme managers to disseminate knowledge on population issues and render it operational. Since the launching of the general awareness-raising programmes among agricultural planners in the 1970s, FAO has developed tools that help policy makers analyse trends in the main determinants of the agricultural resources/requirements equation. Two of the main tools, the Agro-Ecological Zones/Potential Population-Supporting Capacity and the Computerized System for Agriculture and Pop-

ulation Planning and Analysis (CAPP), integrate population data and analytical means to study the impact of population dynamics on prospects for land and agricultural development.

290. Recent years have also seen a growing emphasis on the development of software to sensitize policy makers to the interactions between population and development and their causal mechanisms. Such computer-based programmes help leaders to become aware of the impact of relevant policy interventions. Other software packages have been developed that strengthen national capabilities for future data collection and analysis.

291. The convening of meetings on population has also contributed to increased awareness and greater understanding of population issues. Of particular interest is the case of several conferences of parliamentarians on population issues, which have not only helped governmental officials and the public to gain a better understanding of the relationships between population and development but also strengthened the role of parliamentarians as the crucial link between the Government and the people, in particular as a channel of communication for the articulation of people's needs. Among the important meetings in this regard, the following may be mentioned: the Third Conference of the Asian Forum of Parliamentarians on Population and Development (1990); the Second Western Hemisphere Parliamentarians Conference on Population and Development (1990); the First Asian Women Parliamentarians Conference on Population and Development (1990); and the Fifth and Sixth Asian Parliamentarian Meetings (1989, 1990).

292. Another important meeting that took place in the recent past was the above-mentioned International Forum on Population in the Twenty-first Century (UNFPA, 1990), in which delegates from 79 countries participated. It was a notable international gathering that focused the world's attention on the significance of global population growth. The Forum adopted by consensus the Amsterdam Declaration on a Better Life for Future Generations which laid down a blueprint for needed urgent action in the population field. The Declaration was noted with appreciation by the General Assembly at its forty-fourth session, in resolution 44/210.

293. With the advent of UNFPA's programme review and strategy development (PRSD) exercises in developing countries, signifying a new approach to population programming, the importance of comprehensive information, education and communication strategies has become increasingly evident. The need for such strategies, and for the coordination they imply, is accentuated by the need to take action simultaneously on several fronts in order to achieve programme goals. In response to those needs, there has been an increase in the attention given to strategy development and to information, education and communication research in the training carried out for concerned specialists, particularly the development of skills in research, audience segmentation and media mix. The choice of the medium and target audience and the adaptation of the message to fit local social and cultural realities are increasingly viewed as crucial to the provision of effective population information and education and to effective population-related communication.

294. Another facet of the creation of awareness of population issues is the training of cadres capable of staffing population units and interpreting demographic data to decision makers. The previously existing and newly created regional population training centres have provided relevant training to national experts. UNFPA's Global Programme of Training in Population and Development has also expanded to provide training in the Spanish language and will soon transfer the French-language course to a site in western sub-Saharan Africa.

295. Innovative approaches to reaching young people with population messages have, in the past few years, involved organizing painting and other competitions to engage young minds in the critical analysis of the impact of population growth on such issues as the pollution of the environment and the depletion of natural resources, in terms both of survival and of sustainable development, quality of life and availability of food. In addition, the increased involvement of non-governmental and other organizations in the field of youth and population (for example, the Boy Scouts, the Young Women's Christian Association and IPPF) has resulted in a variety of learning activities for youth that have in many cases harnessed the energy of this group and made its members activists in the population field. The facilitation of a two-way dialogue between policy makers and youth organizations has been an important product of this trend.

296. Finally, among the important events contributing to awareness-creation on population matters throughout the world is the annual celebration of World Population Day, on 11 July. It is accompanied by a wide range of activities and special events for groups ranging from parliamentarians and academics to professionals and young people. Another event is the annual presentation of the United Nations Population Award to individuals or institutions who have been chosen to be honoured for their outstanding contributions in the area of increasing awareness of population issues and working towards their resolution.

297. The Programme of Action suggests a more extensive list of priority population issues that should be included in public-awareness campaigns, such as safe motherhood; reproductive health and rights; maternal and child health and family planning; discrimination against females and persons with disabilities; valorization of the girl child; child abuse; violence against women; male responsibility; gender equality; sexually transmitted diseases, including HIV/AIDS; responsible sexual behaviour; teenage pregnancy; racism and xenophobia; ageing populations; and unsustainable consumption and production patterns. It adds that the media should be a major instrument for expanding knowledge and motivation in education campaigns. The Programme of Action stresses further the importance of relying on up-to-date research findings to determine information needs and the most effective culturally acceptable ways of reaching intended audiences. To that end, it points to the need for involving both the intended audiences and the non-traditional media in the design, implementation and monitoring of information, education and communication activities. Furthermore, the Programme of Action specifies the need for enlisting the entertainment media to encourage public discussion of sensitive topics related to the implementation of the Programme of Action. More-

over, it recognizes the potential of print, audiovisual and electronic media for disseminating technical information and for promoting and strengthening the understanding of the relationships between population, consumption, production and sustainable development.

298.   The Programme of Action expands the list of areas in which population specialists should be trained to include the environment. It also expands, with a grass-roots preference, the kinds of influential people who should have access to information on population and sustainable development and related issues and who should promote an understanding of those issues and mobilize public opinion in support of the actions proposed. In addition to their continued promotion of public awareness on issues related to population and sustainable development, members of parliament are invited to ensure the enactment of legislation necessary for the effective implementation of the Programme of Action.

NOTES

[1]Other periodical publications of the United Nations that systematically include substantive analyses of population issues are the annual *World Economic Survey* and the *Report on the World Social Situation.*

[2]According to the British Broadcasting Corporation, between 1985 and 1991, the number of television receivers increased by 57 per cent in Latin America, 81 per cent in sub-Saharan Africa, 95 per cent in the Arab world, 168 per cent in China (tripling in six years), and 1,639 per cent in India (almost doubling every year).

XI. TECHNOLOGY, RESEARCH AND DEVELOPMENT

299.   Demographic data of sufficient quantity and quality are a prerequisite for the formulation and implementation of appropriate population policies. Population issues must be properly documented and interpreted; otherwise, policy makers and programme officers will not be able to perceive their importance and urgency, understand their determinants and identify the actions that are required to address them. For this reason, the collection, analysis and research of population and other socio-economic variables constitutes a fundamental part of the process that embraces the identification of issues, the formulation and implementation of policies and programmes, and the evaluation of action. The present chapter concentrates on two particular issues—data collection, and substantive and operational research.

Issue No. 23.   Balanced programmes of data collection

300.   The Plan of Action (paras. 72-77) and Mexico City recommendations 60-68 provide extremely useful guidance in the area of data collection and analysis and have been translated into important improvements. At present, for virtually every country in the world, there is available a set of basic indicators, actual and estimated, or projected, on population trends. Those basic indicators include population size, distribution by sex and urban/rural residence, and rates of increase, crude death and birth rates, total fertility rates, infant and child mortality and life expectancy at birth. These data correspond to estimates and projections covering the period 1950-2025. Estimates and projections on internal and international migration are almost non-existent in the majority of countries, and in the area of maternal mortality, where accuracy requires complete civil registration of mortality statistics, only recently has attention been focused on improving those statistics for countries that lack them. For the past two decades, many countries have made progress in obtaining demographic data, including data disaggregated by gender through censuses, surveys and civil registration/vital statistics systems. However, owing to the scarcity of statistics on the environment, it is difficult to assess fully the interaction between population, development and the environment. There is also insufficient utilization of data disaggregation by gender in many countries and some countries do not make such disaggregation available.

301.   In relation to the data originating from population censuses, there have been important improvements in the past 20 years. During the 1980s, 192 countries or areas took a census; in particular, the African Census Programme (50 out of 54 countries participating) and the 1982 Population Census of China were both taken. The decade 1985-1994 was designated by the United Nations as the 1990 census decade. The 1990 World Population and

Housing Census Programme was launched in 1985. In the present decade, 206 countries or areas have carried out or are planning to carry out a population and housing census. In some countries, census preparations had actually been undertaken but for various reasons the census was postponed to a date after 1994 or cancelled. In other countries, population registers and administrative records systems were used to provide census-type data on population and housing. By the end of 1994, it is expected that 96 per cent of the world population will have been enumerated.

302.   Since the 1990 census decade has been witnessing a wide use of microcomputers in the processing and dissemination of data, the United Nations has responded by preparing various publications to assist countries in planning and using centralized and decentralized methods for census processing and tabulation. The use of microcomputers has also facilitated the development of local census statistics for analysis of population trends and characteristics for policy purposes.

303.   Furthermore, a wide range of technical cooperation activities, funded by UNFPA and other donors, were carried out during the past two decades in a large number of developing countries in connection with the successful completion of their national censuses. Those activities included the provision of census experts; advisory services; equipment (including computer hardware and software); and a series of training workshops at both the regional and the national levels. The training workshops covered, *inter alia*, advanced techniques in census cartography, census planning, sampling procedures, methods for collecting economic statistics, data processing, and database development. Of particular importance was a census training programme for sub-Saharan Africa that was funded by the Government of Canada under multi/bilateral arrangements with UNFPA and executed by the Department for Economic and Social Information and Policy Analysis of the United Nations Secretariat, with ECA as the associate executing agency.

304.   Another area that receives attention in the Plan of Action is the establishment of national vital statistics systems (para. 75). The continuing implementation of the World Programme for the Improvement of Vital Statistics was intensified with the launching of the International Programme for Accelerating the Improvement of Vital Statistics and Civil Registration Systems, in 1991. The International Programme was co-sponsored by the Statistical Division of the United Nations Secretariat, UNFPA, WHO and the International Institute for Vital Registration and Statistics. A series of workshops were held in the ECLAC, ESCAP and ESCWA regions, and two others are planned in Africa. Other activities include the preparation and dissemination of several methodological reports and studies for assisting countries to assess the current situation and to implement needed reforms and measures for achieving complete coverage and timeliness of registration and vital statistics.

305.   Migration (both internal and international, but especially international) has been receiving considerable attention. Migration statistics are very deficient, even in the more developed regions. Mexico City recommendation 64 identified migration as the least developed area of current demographic sta-

tistics. Only part of the problem is related to lack of data; even when data exist, there are difficulties in terms of concepts, definitions and classifications of migrants. Therefore, a rational strategy in this area should include a revision of definitions and classifications and of the preparation of guidelines for the collection, tabulation, publication and dissemination of data gathered from multiple sources (population censuses, sample surveys and administrative record systems). Concrete steps in this direction have been taken by the Organisation for Economic Cooperation and Development with the establishment of the Continuous Reporting System on Migration (SOPEMI) which details the evolution of international migration flows to and from its member States and their relevant policies.

306. The *Demographic Yearbook of the United Nations*, an annual publication, has been disseminating a variety of demographic and social statistics over the past four decades. Those data, which exist on a mainframe computer, have been made available on computer tapes, on an ad hoc basis, to private clients, national offices and other users in the international system. In recent years, as microcomputers have become more widespread, the demand for demographic data on microcomputer media has increased. In order to meet these needs, a three-year project has been undertaken to strengthen the existing database. Upon completion, the database will contain time-series on demographic and social statistics since 1950 and will permit their rapid retrieval and efficient use for international population research, including the study of special population groups.

307. Distinct improvements in the area of sample surveys have been made in the past two decades. For example, the World Fertility Survey (WFS), the largest social survey ever undertaken, was launched in 1972. It was carried out by the International Statistical Institute, in collaboration with the United Nations and the International Union for the Scientific Study of Population (IUSSP), with the financial support of UNFPA, the United States Agency for International Development (USAID) and the Overseas Development Administration (United Kingdom). WFS produced not only a set of comparable data covering 20 developed and 42 developing countries but also manuals on survey design, training to nationals of participating countries, data-processing software, standard data tapes and a series of illustrative analyses. When it ended in 1984, the Institute for Resource Development of Macro Systems launched the programme of Demographic and Health Surveys (DHS), which is considered the successor to WFS surveys. On a smaller scale, in the context of the National Household Survey Capability Programme (NHSCP), the United Nations, in collaboration with UNICEF, UNFPA and IPPF, and with financial assistance from the Arab Gulf Programme for United Nations Development Organizations (AGFUND), has been undertaking a project called the Pan-Arab Project for Child Development (PAPCHILD) which is aimed at the collection of data on health for policy and programming.

308. Several activities have been designed to address special population groups, such as children, persons with disabilities, and the elderly. Such activities include, *inter alia:*

(a) Development of concepts, definitions and classifications;

(*b*)   Design of strategies for data collection and the development of international databases;

(*c*)   Preparing of training manuals and handbooks; and

(*d*)   Technical cooperation activities, including training workshops and advisory services.

With respect to people with disabilities, notable advances have been made in data compilation and dissemination. The international Disability Statistics Database (DISTAT) comprises 12 major socio-economic and demographic topics concerning disability.

309.   The implementation and the monitoring of international instruments related to the full integration of women into society on an equal basis with men require a solid data foundation. Of particular interest has been the preparation of the Women's Indicators and Statistics Database (WISTAT) and *The World's Women, 1970-1990: Trends and Statistics* (United Nations, 1990). WISTAT is an integrated, readily available, comprehensive database for microcomputers.

310.   The above account shows that some important successes have been achieved in the area of data collection; nevertheless, much work remains to be done. Indeed, in many developing countries, basic data are deficient and incomplete; analyses based on current direct observations are still lacking; the institutional basis for the collection, processing and dissemination of statistical information is weak; and, in particular, there is a need for improving the quality of human resources committed to these activities. It has become clear that the data collected from censuses, civil registration systems, household surveys and other sources can be considered complete only when they have been evaluated, disseminated and analysed so as to provide demographic knowledge concerning trends and their socio-economic correlates. Although each system of data collection has its merits, it becomes more valuable when complemented by others. In this respect, the third review and appraisal of the Plan of Action concluded that a balanced programme of data collection and analysis for any given country would aim at gradual and harmonious improvement in the different systems of collection and analysis which would fit the particular conditions of the country, and that such a programme should consider particular information needs in terms of specific groups of the population (United Nations, 1989b).

311.   Beyond previous recommendations regarding technology, research and development, the Programme of Action recommends that data collection should take into account ethical and legal standards and be carried out in consultation and partnership with local communities and institutions; that comparability be ensured in all research and data collection programmes; that findings be made accessible and available to policy makers, decision makers, planners and managers of programmes for timely use; and that interaction between data users and data providers be promoted. It also recommends that comprehensive and reliable qualitative as well as quantitative databases be established, allowing linkages between population, education, health, poverty, family well-being, environment and development issues, and providing information disaggregated at appropriate and desired levels. The databases should

be maintained by countries to meet the needs of research and of policy and programme development, implementation, monitoring and evaluation; and suitable indicators should be developed. In addition, relevant information networks should be created or strengthened at the national, regional and global levels.

Issue No. 24. *Substantive and operational research*

312. The Plan of Action (paras. 78-80) and Mexico City recommendations 69-72 give strong emphasis to research activities relating to population and identify the priority areas needing research to fill gaps in knowledge. As part of the preparatory activities for the 1994 International Conference on Population and Development, six expert group meetings were convened to discuss various population issues, provide a substantive basis for assessing the Plan of Action, address the issues of the coming decade, and recommend action. Each of the meetings examined the level of understanding of particular issues and identified gaps and limitations. Many of the conclusions have been valuable in the preparation of the present report.

313. The principal areas covered by research during the past two decades ranged from social, cultural and economic determinants of population variables in different developmental and political situations to social indicators reflecting the quality of life and the interrelationships between socioeconomic and demographic phenomena. Renewed attention has also been paid to population, environment and development issues, which had already figured prominently in the preparations for the World Population Conference in 1974. During the same period there was gathered a significantly large body of qualitative and quantitative information obtained from a worldwide research effort. There have also been major advances in the research of census, survey and registration methods used in the collection of such qualitative and quantitative information and in the dissemination of information and research results to users. A review of recent research reveals shifts in emphasis among the different research areas and points to important advances and gaps that require further research.

314. Important research work has been carried out at the interregional and regional levels. Studies in this area have focused on the interrelationships between socio-economic and population variables, population and development, and the demographic aspects of development planning. At the country level, research has given particular emphasis to the analysis of population growth, population distribution and the determinants and consequences of migration, migration and unemployment, and human resource development. Although considerable research has been carried out, an array of research questions, especially at the operational level, remain to be addressed in specific country situations. In general, it should be recognized that the research infrastructure in many developing countries is weak, particularly in the least developed countries. In many cases, research has been "donor driven" and has not involved the national officers who are expected to apply the results of research to their programmes. A paucity of human and financial resources has contributed to this situation.

315. Recent trends in the analysis of population dynamics have shifted from fact-finding studies to more focused analyses of how population issues are integrated into socio-economic development planning and programming. A trend in recent years, and one likely to gain momentum in the future, is the growing recognition of the importance of policy-oriented research on socio-cultural factors affecting human reproductive behaviour, not only in relation to reproduction but also as regards morbidity, mortality, migration and urbanization. The International Forum on Population in the Twenty-first Century recommended an expansion of research to encompass the determinants of fertility and family planning attitudes and behaviour, family relationships, sexual behaviour and cultural barriers impeding the integration of women in the overall development process (UNFPA, 1990).

316. The Programme of Action stresses the urgent need for research on sexuality and gender roles and relationships to be conducted in different cultural settings. It also stresses the need to involve women at all stages of gender research planning and to recruit and train more female researchers. In addition, it highlights areas that need emphasis, such as abuse, discrimination and violence against women; genital mutilation, where practised; sexual behaviour and mores; male attitudes towards sexuality and procreation, fertility, family and gender roles; risk-taking behaviour regarding sexually transmitted diseases and unplanned pregnancies; women's and men's perceived needs for methods for regulation of fertility and sexual health services; and reasons for non-use or ineffective use of existing services and technologies.

317. Research efforts on the interactions between population and the environment over the past 20 years have, on the one hand, sought, with varying degrees of success, to create macrolevel analytical frameworks and, on the other, applied themselves to empirical investigations at the microlevel. Perhaps the most critical shortfall exists in the area of empirical microlevel studies of particular localities. However, a number of potentially significant projects at both levels are being undertaken at present, reflecting the renewed interest on issues of long-term sustainability, highlighted by the United Nations Conference on Environment and Development. The study on the relationship between population pressures, poverty and environmentally endangered zones is a field of research that should be given high priority in the coming years.

318. Over the past 20 years the topic of migration has been perceived to be an increasingly crucial demographic and political problem. Spurred by the paucity of research on both internal and international migration, research on migration has been growing very fast, being focused mainly on the analysis of present and future emigration pressures on the developed countries. Relatively little research exists, however, on movements between developing countries. There is also a lack of serious research on refugees, particularly in the developing countries.

319. In recent years, increasing attention has been given to the ageing of populations in many countries. This demographic trend is considered to have significant economic and social implications which vary considerably according to country-specific circumstances. They include the effects of ageing on

pensions, the labour force, medical care, family structure and residential patterns. The focus of research on age structure has not been limited to the growth of the elderly population but has considered age distribution in its entirety in a broad framework of global and historical changes. Much research attention has been paid to the causes of change in age structure and its consequences for public revenue and expenditure and the labour force and to the identification of possible adjustment mechanisms and approaches to improving demographic policies.

320.   Research in human reproduction, with specific focus on the needs of developing countries, has been expanding. During recent years, considerable progress has been made in the area of research, development and assessment of fertility-regulating methods, including methods for use by men, although practical applications are not expected until some years into the future.

321.   In the past few years, the role of men in fertility, and particularly male responsibility for family planning, has become an important research topic. More studies, however, need to be done, especially at the operational level, to discover effective means of involving male partners in family planning decisions. The investigation of operational questions such as these has been taken up by several national non-governmental organizations which probably have a comparative advantage by virtue of their grass-roots character.

322.   In spite of a considerable amount of operational research carried out on the provision of family planning services, needs in this area are still great because of the growing demand for cost-effectiveness and self-financing of programmes in the face of increasing financial constraints. Operational research and specific micro-level surveys have yielded many operational answers to programmatic questions about service delivery, including quality of care, sociocultural sensitivities, women's needs and more effective cost-recovery strategies. Nevertheless, in many cases, operational research has been limited and is rarely institutionalized as part of delivery systems.

323.   At the operational level, recent research has branched into several specific topics designed to improve the quality and accessibility of family-planning services. An international programme to estimate contraceptive requirements to the year 2000 has made good progress and helped the coordination of international efforts in contraceptive commodities procurement, although more efforts in this area are needed if the expected growth in demand in developing countries is to be met in the next few years. More systematic research into the legal impediments to family planning practice, ranging from import restrictions to civil laws affecting, for example, availability of contraceptives to adolescents has also accelerated in recent years.

324.   The Programme of Action further recommends that both male and female barrier methods, microbicides and virucides receive increased attention in reproductive health research, both for fertility control and for the prevention of sexually transmitted diseases, including HIV/AIDS. It also stresses the need to give high priority to the development of new methods for male fertility regulation and to research the factors inhibiting male involvement and responsibility in family planning. In order to expedite the availability of improved and new methods for the regulation of fertility, the Programme of Ac-

tion urges that efforts be made to increase the involvement of industry and to encourage a partnership between the public and private sectors in order to mobilize the experience and resources of industry while protecting the public interest. It adds the need to ensure that both national and international ethical and technical standards are met in the development process of contraceptive drugs and devices and that the user's perspective be incorporated in the process. The Programme of Action urges developed countries to assist research programmes in developing countries and countries with economies in transition with their knowledge, experience and technical expertise add promote the transfer of appropriate technologies to them and the international community in order to facilitate local production of contraceptive commodities in developing countries and countries with economies in transition.

325.   In the area of health, recent research has focused on maternal mortality, maternal and reproductive morbidity and assessments of unmet needs for family planning. Important advances have been made in the understanding of the interactions between family planning, maternal mortality and child survival. Epidemiological and operational research remains a vital instrument in the efforts to reduce maternal morbidity and mortality. The Programme of Action points out that in conducting sexual and reproductive health research, special attention should be given to the needs of adolescents in order to develop suitable policies and programmes and appropriate technologies to meet their health needs. Special priority should also be given to research on sexually transmitted diseases, including HIV/AIDS, and to research on fertility.

326.   In the next decade, further research will be needed for the development and adaptation of the appropriate technologies and methodologies necessary to reduce high levels of severe morbidity and maternal mortality and for the investigation of their underlying causes.

327.   Recent years have seen emphasis on the development of methods for making rapid assessments of social and economic events that are important in understanding the interaction between population and development, providing substantive and technical bases for policy-relevant research, and establishing quick baselines for the evaluation of programme efforts.

328.   Numerous socio-cultural research studies conducted during the past 20 years have made considerable contributions to the development of information, education and communication activities. However, there is still a lack of knowledge about the socio-cultural and psychological profiles of specific target groups, including cultural acceptability of the concept of contraception and the specific methods for achieving it. Among other key areas for future studies is research on socio-cultural factors affecting demographic behaviour in urban squatter settlements. Disaggregation of quantitative and qualitative information by gender, essential for socio-cultural research, has advanced in recent years but remains inadequate.

329.   Another important challenge confronting researchers is to make the best possible use of the microcomputers that are becoming widely available. Microcomputer technology has now been used extensively in assisting the collection, processing, organization, storage and analysis of population information. The dissemination of a large quantity of complex data to users

through magnetic means, to supplement traditional printed publications, can be carried out effectively. The use of microcomputers could contribute greatly to the decentralization of research to subnational levels, which would thus become more programme-oriented; but achieving this will require methodological and substantive work at all levels.

330.   Among the issues that merit more attention and further investigation in the area of population and development are the following linkages: the effect of population growth on the ability to increase human resource investments; poor governance in the face of mounting population pressures; unsustainable efforts to increase food production; strains on water resources; and costs associated with a lower versus a higher degree of population stabilization.

XII. NATIONAL ACTION

331. The World Population Plan of Action recognizes the sovereign right of countries to respond to their own population and development issues and affirms that the success of the Plan of Action will largely depend on the actions undertaken by national Governments (para. 96). In this sense, the ultimate responsibility for action or inaction in population matters belongs to national Governments. Action undertaken by countries to address their population problems, in a broadened context of social and economic development, encompasses a large variety of activities to be carried out by many different actors, such as national government ministries and agencies, regional and local authorities, legislators, non-governmental organizations and the private sector, local communities, families, couples and individuals. In an increasing number of countries, Governments have recently been modifying the manner in which they manage their national affairs, in particular by giving greater recognition to the larger role to be played by market forces and private initiatives, as opposed to public regulation. National Governments, when making collective decisions and choices, tend more and more to foster the participation of the different actors that constitute the social web of nations. This chapter concentrates on three key issues: the integration of population concerns into development planning and programming; the management of programmes; and the achievement of self-reliance.

Issue No. 25. Integrated approaches for population policies

332. Comprehensive population policies facilitate the consideration of the various relationships between population factors and socio-economic development in a manner that minimizes policy contradictions and promotes internally consistent and harmonious development. Beginning in the early 1960s, many developing countries started to be involved in preparing their plans and strategies for social and economic development. In many instances, population was included in the planning process, at least as a reference point for defining the current and projected magnitude of needs and resources.

333. The Plan of Action states, in its principles and objectives, that population and development are interrelated: population variables influence development variables and are also influenced by them (para. 14 (c)). In recognition of these linkages, the Plan of Action recommends that population measures and programmes should be integrated into comprehensive social and economic plans and programmes and that this integration should be reflected in the goals, instrumentalities and organizations for planning within the countries. It is suggested that in general a unit dealing with population aspects be created and placed at a high level of the national administrative structure and that such a unit be staffed with qualified persons from the relevant disciplines (para. 95).

334.   According to information in the Population Policy Data Bank, the vast majority of Governments at present have units responsible for taking into account population variables in development planning within their central planning or programming agencies. A large proportion of the developing countries (more than 75 per cent) have a national development plan currently in effect, and two thirds of the Governments have at least one agency for formulating or coordinating population policies and a unit for taking into account population variables in development planning within the central planning agency.

335.   In recent years, considerable efforts have been made to establish institutional mechanisms to heighten awareness of population issues and to lobby for effective resolution of those issues. Many developing countries have organized national population commissions or councils that are high-level governmental bodies. These councils or commissions are usually charged with the responsibility for making decisions or giving advice on population matters in general or for spearheading the formulation of population policies and coordinating all population programmes in the public and private sectors. In many cases, these commissions are also charged with the responsibility of channelling financial and technical assistance for population programmes. The location and effectiveness of these commissions and councils are influenced by the degree of national commitment to population and development issues.

336.   In addition to these commissions or councils, there are also population units in planning, health and education ministries in over 70 developing countries. Those commissions, councils and units, by formulating comprehensive population policies, have played a leading role in legitimizing the idea that population is also a programmable sector, and in promoting the acceptance of population activities. In many countries where commissions or councils exist, the population units act as technical secretariats.

337.   Considerable efforts have been made to assist national Governments in organizing and equipping the units in order effectively to undertake and promote research, policy development, programming, and coordination activities. A variety of training programmes have been used—*inter alia*, on-the-job training assisted by full-time international experts and consultants and the provision of practical methodological tools, including microcomputer-based user-friendly software (with training provided for their use), and administrative and logistical support. Similar efforts have been made in relation to national research institutions.

338.   Beyond the considerations presented above, evaluating international progress on the integration of population into development policies and vice versa appears to be as difficult as the task of integrating population into development planning itself. This area of the Plan of Action seems to have received less attention than many others, in spite of its recognized importance. One reason for the relative lack of attention is uncertainty concerning the meaning of the term "integration", which may be used to refer to different concerns, involving:

(a)   The use of demographic data to project the size of various groups likely to demand specific services (school-age child labour, the elderly and so on);

(b)   The recognition that policies designed for a given purpose (for example, increased spending on the education of women and girls to improve the labour force and raise household incomes) might produce a significant impact on certain population variables (for example, in this case, perhaps the lowering of fertility);

(c)   The modelling of the linkages and feedback mechanisms between economic, social and demographic variables when development strategies are being prepared.

All of the above types of integration can be found in the multitude of national planning experiences around the world, although the third type is most in line with the ideal type of integration envisioned by the Plan of Action.

339.   In addition to the intellectual difficulty of defining integration, there are also problems related to the implementation of population policies. Among those problems, the most common is determining the exact linkages between population and development and then developing techniques for modelling them. Another reason for the insufficient progress is the weak level of communication between policy makers and researchers; a more effective constructive dialogue between them would help the identification of options for policy-making and programming decisions. Other key problems are the unavailability of trained human resources for such sophisticated analyses and the difficulty of collecting necessary data on demographic, economic and social variables. Information from the Population Policy Data bank indicates that more than half of the Governments in the developing countries regard the following factors as obstacles to the integration of population variables into the development planning process: lack of appropriate methods for assessing the data they have; inadequacy of data on the linkages between population and development; and lack of trained personnel.

340.   Sub-Saharan Africa is likely to remain the priority region for population planning. Population problems (especially rapid population growth, refugee and other migration issues, urbanization and spatial distribution) and their complex interactions with such factors as poverty, underemployment and environmental degradation and the effective implementation of national population policies deserve continued attention and support. Most countries in sub-Saharan Africa have weak analytical and planning capacities, and only recently have they begun to recognize that demographic and related factors play a crucial role in the development process, and hence that active intervention policies may be required. Over the past decade or so, a great deal of effort has gone into the establishment of the minimum conditions necessary for integrated planning in those countries. Sensitization activities designed to create awareness have formed a major component of the international assistance provided by the United Nations system, with the aim of building a national consensus so that designing public policy could become population-oriented.

341.   In contrast to sub-Saharan African countries, many Asian and Latin American countries have already relatively developed analytical and

institutional capacities for planning. As far as Asia is concerned, there is also a well-established tradition of intervention in the population field. These are countries where the conditions for effective integrated planning have largely been met. Their needs for technical assistance are more specialized and refer to areas such as sectoral planning, migration and urbanization, incorporation of gender concerns into policy, specific policy advice on such issues as population and the environment, and technical aspects of modelling and the use of advanced software packages. Many of those countries also need assistance for undertaking planning at the subnational level.

342.   Many countries in Northern Africa and Western Asia may be placed in between the other two groups. They have relatively developed analytical and planning capacities but, as in the first group, population issues tend to receive inadequate attention in public policy. Thus, the initial requirement is to create favourable conditions for taking proper account of population factors in human resource development strategies and programmes—for example, through the establishment and strengthening of population units and through sensitization activities.

343.   In many countries, mainly outside Africa, population and human resource development policies and activities have often been undertaken in the absence of a comprehensive framework. Indeed, efforts have at times been limited to the pursuit of population-influencing strategies and, particularly, family planning. While such an approach may have the advantage of focusing attention and scarce resources on very specific priorities, it may lead to the neglect of some otherwise important population-responsive policies. Exclusively population-influencing policies may backfire or have unanticipated effects—for example, individual resistance to family planning programmes is sometimes based on a perception that such programmes represent governmental interference with private decisions.

344.   The experience gained in the implementation of technical cooperation projects in the area of integration of population into development shows a great diversity in terms of analytical and planning capacities among regions. Two crucial conditions must be met if integrated population and development planning is to be achieved. The first is that a political climate in which population issues are considered central to public policy be created. A major step towards the achievement of such a political climate is the organization of activities that sensitize and create awareness, targeted at all levels of opinion formation and decision-making and reaching down ultimately to the general population. The second crucial condition is that an adequate institutional and technical capacity be created. The experience gained in the past two decades indicates that a major means for attempting to achieve such integration is the establishment and/or strengthening of the population units mentioned above. Those units should be composed of an adequate number of competent personnel, linked to key policy-making bodies and to other relevant ministries, having access to basic demographic and socio-economic data and to analytical tools and planning methodologies that can be adapted to suit local conditions.

345. Countries that have recently adopted or are in the process of formulating national population policies require substantial assistance in the preparation and implementation of detailed and well-coordinated global and sectoral action plans. Their needs go well beyond technical advice. To make an informed choice between alternative instruments and strategies, planners and decision makers need to have an idea of the level of resources that can be made available, *inter alia*, for the development and implementation of specific measures and programmes and for the setting up of coordination, monitoring and evaluation mechanisms. A high degree of commitment to population policy implementation is therefore essential.

346. The information presented above does indicate that there are indeed serious barriers to be overcome in the integration of population variables into the development planning process, but it also points to ways of overcoming those barriers. Recommendations concerning ways in which the institutions of the United Nations system can help overcome the obstacles include mention of the following:

(*a*) Continued support for institutional capacity-building in developing country Governments, including data collection, research and analysis;

(*b*) Training programmes focusing on appropriate methods for modelling the linkages between economic, social and demographic factors;

(*c*) Further research into the mechanisms through which population and development variables are linked;

(*d*) Policy dialogue in support of the establishment of agencies devoted to the integration of population and development for those countries that do not yet have them, and of the improvement of those agencies in countries that already have them.

Issue No. 26. Management of programmes

347. Self-reliance, achieved by building the capacity of Governments, non-governmental organizations and the private sector to address the population issues of their countries, requires the participation of skilled workers and the establishment of a proper administrative environment. The Plan of Action (para. 81) and particularly the Mexico City recommendations (para. 36 and recommendations 73 and 77) recognize such needs and suggest establishing monitoring and evaluation systems, strengthening administrative and managerial capacity and involving communities more actively. More precisely, the International Conference on Population focused on three main specifications for the management of population programmes:

(*a*) Management should be strengthened through appropriate training activities;

(*b*) All regional and interregional agencies and national Governments should lend their full support to the management of population programmes, and national Governments should seek ways of promoting technical cooperation among developing countries, paying special attention to training of trainers and emphasizing women's participation in all phases of the process;

(c) Raising awareness should be sought through special programmes for decision makers, administrators, media communicators and other relevant actors.

348. In the past two decades, efforts to improve the management of population programmes have taken many forms, including reorganizing programme structures; establishing new systems of monitoring and decision-making; improving management training; upgrading service delivery and its support services with a view to enhancing quality of care; and improving logistics and management information systems. International organizations, donors, Governments and non-governmental organizations are making efforts to tailor training activities to meet the specific requirements of programmes. There is also a great opportunity for successful technical cooperation among developing countries in the area of population programme management.

349. These efforts have, in many cases, been hampered by human, financial and technical resources constraints. Many Governments, for example, need to recruit local programme management personnel for their maternal and child health care and family planning (MCH/FP) programmes from among those who, although they have already demonstrated their abilities in managing public and/or private sector programmes in other areas, do not have prior experience in MCH/FP activities.

350. Although there has been some progress in integrating gender concerns into programme planning and programme management, much more needs to be done to ensure the full incorporation of gender issues into population programmes. A number of programmes in the area of MCH/FP and in information, education and communication, which are generally addressed mainly to women, have been found to be seriously deficient because the specific needs of women were not considered in project design and implementation. Women have not always been consulted or asked to participate in the identification of needs, programme development and management, and decision-making.

351. The Management of family planning programmes, already difficult in many countries, is often made more so by a lack of adequate managerial training. Although women constitute the majority of health-care providers in many societies, they seldom occupy managerial-level positions in the health and family planning system. There is particular need for women-centred and women-managed facilities so as to ensure that their MCH/FP needs are taken fully into consideration.

352. The area of training has been signalled as a major concern. In many cases, national project personnel, although given responsibility for a wide variety of tasks, have received little management training. Top managers often lack specialized management skills and training. Rapid changes in management and administrative technology have, in some cases, fostered a dependence on international experts. The management of population programmes continues to demand the recruitment of good managers and the development of managerial skills through well-planned training. The aim should be to maintain and expand a critical mass of high-level administrators of population programmes.

353. Responding to this need, training programmes have been designed to strengthen the management capabilities of family planning organizations, with particular emphasis on improving quality and access to services. While some progress has been made in inserting appropriate public administration and management components into the training of some population specialists and although some skills in this area are being built among population scientists, the inclusion of relevant population themes in the curricula of public administration and management programmes has been less successful. Yet, without such expertise and conviction on the part of public administrators, well-founded population concerns will continue to remain largely restricted to academic circles. Therefore, special curricula focusing on population issues, designed to meet the needs of public administrators and managers, should be urgently developed. In designing such programmes, special attention should be paid to the multisectoral nature of population issues.

354. Another area where action has been slow is the identification of the actual managerial needs of population programmes. It is not enough to emphasize the substantive and academic skills that are required for further programme development and enhancement; due attention must be paid to the managerial instruments that are needed to run programmes in a more effective fashion.

355. It was indicated, in relation to issue No. 23 above, that in the area of data collection and analysis, many developing countries have reached some form of self-reliance. However, what needs to be strengthened further is the managerial components of the dissemination of data and the results of analyses and the promotion of data-user services. Regarding the incorporation of population elements into national and sectoral development plans and programmes, while many Governments have become increasingly aware of those elements, methodologies, tools and measures are still lacking and, where they exist, are weak. Hence, further work in this area is critical.

356. One of the most important issues facing managers and administrators is the expansion and improvement of family planning services. Countries with a high success rate in expanding the accessibility and reach of their delivery systems have been successful largely by improving contraceptive logistics and utilizing private-sector efficiency at the local and national levels, although the importance of the private sector varies considerably among relatively successful programmes in different regions. Experience has shown that even minimum strategic interventions on a broad scale will most likely lead to the success of country population programmes when they are accompanied by improvements in the quality of services and increased community participation. In the case of family planning, strategic management should give priority to improving the distribution of a broad range of contraceptive methods, monitoring of contraception continuation rates, raising the quality of services by making them more sensitive to client needs, and promoting gender balance in senior management positions. There is also a growing recognition that sustained political commitment and cooperation among all relevant governmental and non-governmental personnel and institutions are key components in managing population programmes.

357. The inadequate development or use of management information systems has been identified as an important obstacle to effective management of national population programmes, particularly MCH/FP programmes, around the world. Several programmatic and managerial issues regarding management information systems in support of MCH/FP programmes were identified during the UNFPA diagnostic surveys conducted in Africa, Asia and Latin America and the Caribbean in 1989. Those issues included, among others, lack of focus on management-related indicators; lack of feedback to local levels; lack of accuracy and timeliness of information; and the shortage of trained personnel for interpreting and analysing MIS data for planning and management of family-planning programmes.

358. Attempts to improve management information systems in the area of family planning have included efforts to simplify existing systems so that they provide accurate and timely information and to provide training for management, supervisory and service personnel in the correct production and use of information. The challenge in the coming years will be to develop and implement inexpensive and easy-to-use management information systems for monitoring the quality and quantity of programme performance and impact.

359. Another common managerial problem is the lack of organizational clarity concerning which governmental bodies have responsibility for population programmes. Such imprecision has adversely affected the administration and management of population programmes. Many programmes are also faced with problems in internal management, field and client relations, relations with other sectors of the Government, and proper management of political linkages with international agencies.

360. Improving the quality of services has become a major concern in the management of programmes. The target-oriented approach of many family planning programmes in the past has contributed to several problems: high discontinuation rates; excessive reliance on non-reversible contraceptive methods; persistence of high rates of induced abortion; and, in some cases, an excessively unbalanced sex ratio, owing to son preference. In the 1990s, attention has turned away from the target-oriented to the quality-oriented approach in family planning services. Recent studies have shown that, wherever management offered a genuine choice of methods, with good information and counselling, there were fewer drop-outs and more satisfied users. The consensus is that satisfied users are not only the key to high continuation rates but also the most effective promoters of family planning. Programme managers should therefore make continuous strategic improvements in the quality of care, because such improvements will not only help users to achieve their reproductive goals but, by doing so, will also promote higher contraceptive prevalence and lead to reductions in fertility. Managing and improving quality services will require a genuine commitment at all levels of management to offering services of high quality and to striving for a better understanding of clients' needs and preferences.

361. UNFPA has, in recent years, given serious attention to improving not only its management strategies for field operations, but also its own internal management. The Governing Council of UNDP noted that by 1990 sev-

eral steps had been taken to strengthen UNFPA's programme management capability: an improvement in the procedures for the recruitment of staff; rotation of staff between the field and headquarters; greater emphasis on confidence-building within the organization; and the increased self-decentralization of decision-making to the field. UNFPA's leadership has also taken steps to expand technical support at the regional level through the Technical Support System (TSS) and by improving strategic planning in country programmes through the above-mentioned programme review and strategy development country missions. Such innovations have significant potential to increase the effectiveness of country-level operations.

362. In conclusion, the experience of the past 20 years indicates that good management is a key factor in determining the success or failure of population programmes. To improve the managerial capacities of countries with respect to operating their population programmes, particular attention should be given to improving the quality of their human resources; establishing/ strengthening their management information systems; reorienting their programmes towards a more client-oriented approach; and involving their communities more extensively in the planning and implementation of programmes. In the area of family planning programmes, particular attention should continue to be given to a large variety of tasks, such as improving the availability and accessibility of contraceptive services that are of high quality, affordable and culturally acceptable; providing varied options and approaches for different target groups; providing a broad range of contraceptive methods; raising the quality of services by making them more sensitive to client needs; utilizing appropriate information, education and communication programmes; promoting gender balance in senior management positions; and monitoring and evaluating all programme components on a timely basis.

363. The recommendations of the Programme of Action indicate a sharper focus on the national monitoring of progress towards meeting its goals, albeit in collaboration with the international community and non-governmental organizations. It suggests that in addition to Governments, non-traditional modalities, such as non-governmental organizations, the private sector and local communities, should strive to mobilize and effectively utilize the resources for population and development programmes, while assisted, upon request, by the international community. It further recommends that governmental and non-governmental recipient organizations and international donor organizations should collaborate on figuring cost estimates. In addition, it urges Governments to devote an increased proportion of public-sector expenditures and of official development assistance to the social sectors, focusing in particular on poverty eradication, within the context of sustainable development.

Issue No. 27. Achieving self-reliance

364. As mentioned above, both the Plan of Action and the Mexico City recommendations give explicit recognition to the vital role of independent, sovereign, national action in the population field. At the same time, it is also recognized that national decision makers could face many impediments in this area, including administrative and managerial weakness; a shortage of the hu-

man and capital resources necessary for effective population programme implementation; inadequate monitoring and evaluation systems to provide decision makers with appropriate feedback in order to devise more effective approaches; and lack of adequate mechanisms to ensure that international assistance is provided under arrangements and on conditions that are adapted to the administrative resources of the recipient country (recommendation 77 (c)).

365. The goal of achieving self-reliance has been on the agenda of many major population and development meetings since the conferences at Bucharest in 1974 and at Mexico City 10 years later. In 1984, for example, African Governments in the Kilimanjaro Programme of Action[1], proposed accelerating self-reliant, social and economic development for the well-being of African peoples. In 1992, African Governments noted that, despite the increased number of explicit population policies formulated in the continent, the implementation rate of the Kilimanjaro Programme had remained low, and they reiterated the call for self-reliance in the draft Dakar/Ngor declaration on population, family and sustainable development (ECA, 1992). Similar proposals were made by other regional meetings. More recently, the Tenth Conference of Heads of State and Government of the Non-Aligned Movement (Jakarta, Indonesia, September 1992) called for an early ministerial meeting on population of the non-aligned movement. The meeting took place in 1993 and considered a series of means to achieve self-reliance that include

(a) The intensification of exchange of information regarding member countries' experience with population policies and family-planning programmes;

(b) The organization of South/South technical cooperation and assistance agreements with respect to education and awareness-raising activities, safe motherhood and family planning programmes;

(c) The establishment of joint cooperation for the production of medical supplies required in programmes.[2]

366. In regard to political commitment, countries with strong population policies have typically been able to mobilize sustained commitment not only at the highest level but down to local leaders at the grass-roots level as well. There is also a growing realization that population policies will not be successful and sustainable unless the beneficiaries, especially women, are fully involved in their design and subsequent implementation. The reviews of progress in these areas, carried out in 1984 and 1989, revealed that while significant progress had been made in achieving self-reliance, particularly in countries where there was a strong governmental commitment, in many other developing countries the common responsible factor was the lack of adequate resources.

367. The role of institutions is also crucial in promoting self-reliance in managing population programmes. A significant number of Governments throughout the developing world, as mentioned above, have established population commissions, councils and units. Despite the widespread establishment of those entities, many issues still need to be dealt with. One of the most important is clarifying the mode of interaction between the population unit and sectoral ministries with responsibilities in population-relevant areas. In-

creasingly, the recognition that sound institution-building should be multi-sectoral, broad-based and extended to the district level has been growing.

368. As noted above, a foundation for national self-reliance in population programming has been established in many countries. In most cases, however, it is a bare beginning and much more needs to be done to better set up and institutionalize national capacity for population programme implementation. The growing collaboration between governmental, non-governmental and regional organizations, the renewed emphasis on people's participation at the community level and the mainstreaming of the role of women in development are all efforts that should be continued.

369. To achieve self-reliance and the integration of population and development planning, there must be a network of local capabilities in the collection, research and analysis of data on the interrelationships between population and development, policy formulation and programme development. Multilateral and bilateral agencies have continued to assist in the development of a national self-reliant capacity to collect, analyse, use and disseminate population-related data. Those efforts have been aimed at enhancing national capacity and self-reliance in formulating, implementing, monitoring and evaluating population policies and programmes. A notable contribution in this direction has been the organization of the programme review and strategy development missions by UNFPA, which aim at the establishment of a concrete strategic framework for a country's population programme on the basis of an in-depth review of the achievements of and the constraints in current population activities and the need for future action.

370. Efforts to better orchestrate and coordinate international assistance have also been strengthened by UNFPA's policy guidelines on national execution. Such efforts are in accord with recent provisions made by the General Assembly (resolution 44/211) which emphasize, *inter alia*, the need to ensure maximum utilization of national capacity through, in particular, government/national execution of projects, a more programme-oriented approach and regular and timely provision of technical advice and backstopping by agencies at the country level. The above provisions led UNFPA to review and expand its technical activities through the new technical support system and to prepare major revisions of the terms of collaboration between UNFPA and other United Nations agencies and non-governmental organizations. Under this revised strategy, considering that the emphasis was to be placed increasingly on the execution of programmes by the Governments themselves, what was sought was to combine such a trend with substantive support to be provided by multidisciplinary teams of specialists, whose location would be at subregional centres in all five major areas of the developing world, bolstered by a thinner layer of agency state-of-the-art specialists located in their respective headquarters. To date, for the activities sponsored by UNFPA, the estimated proportion of projects executed directly by the Governments themselves (execution ratio) for 1993 is 31 per cent, as compared with 25.7 per cent in 1991 and 20.9 per cent in 1992.

371. As part of its effort to enhance the operational activities of the United Nations system, the General Assembly adopted resolution 47/199 in

1992, in which it encouraged greater coordination at the country level. A central aspect of the enhanced coordination is the preparation of a country strategy note by each Government receiving assistance. The note is intended to reflect national priorities and identify ways in which the collaborative approach of agencies within the United Nations system can be used at an advantage and make a distinct difference in meeting the needs of the particular country. A range of United Nations agencies, including UNICEF, UNDP, UNFPA, ILO, FAO, the World Meteorological Organization (WMO) and the International Fund for Agricultural Development (IFAD), contributed to the initial guidelines for the country strategy note concept and organized workshops to help push it forward. It is likely that experience of agencies at the country level, such as that of UNFPA with the Programme Review and Strategy Development (PRSD), will be helpful in this multisectoral approach. Acceptance of the approach is reflected in these statistics: as of October 1994, 62 countries had chosen to prepare a country strategy note, another 62 had not yet taken a final decision, and 7 had chosen not to start the process. It is expected that country strategy notes will focus on areas where the United Nations system can make a significant difference in a concerted team effort.

372.   Information from the Population Policy Data Bank indicates that the majority of countries that have expressed the need for assistance in the field of population during the coming decade have mentioned the area of training in population as a means of achieving self-reliance. Similar findings have been gathered by UNFPA through a number of assessments in the area of training. In fact, the ability of national Governments to achieve self-reliance in managing their population programmes is often constrained by inadequate and insufficient attention to human resource development. This has resulted in weak mechanisms for supervision and control and insufficient attention to staff development and training.

373.   With the increased awareness that human resources development is critical for promoting and enhancing national self-reliance, a growing number of Governments, with the assistance of international agencies and donor organizations, have been giving priority to training issues, especially those relating to the development of administrative capabilities in the population field. Human resource development calls for dynamic partnerships, employing multidisciplinary approaches, between teaching, training and research institutions in academic environments, and governmental, semi-public and community-level agencies involved in planning and policy formulation. It seems reasonably clear that Governments are becoming increasingly self-reliant at the higher professional levels of the population field; hence, the lower overall demand for resident United Nations technical advisers. At the same time, however, the emphasis that continues to be placed on training activities of all kinds, including institution-building and development of permanent in-country training capacities, suggests that the goal of becoming entirely self-reliant in this area is far from having been attained in many countries.

374.   On the basis of the experience gained, it can be concluded that future demands for international assistance will be expressed particularly in the area of training, including the institutionalization of certain training functions within the developing countries themselves. New linkages need to be

fostered between academic training/research institutions and governmental agencies mandated to deal with development planning and population policies and programmes. One particularly important area that requires further attention is training in management itself. Experience has shown that short-term intensive training in management can be highly effective, and some expertise already exists in the specific field of management for population specialists. Much more remains to be done, however, and it is therefore recommended that future efforts be concentrated in this area.

375. The importance of coordinating population activities was stressed in the Plan of Action and the Mexico City recommendations and at recent gatherings such as the Amsterdam International Forum on Population and the Development Assistance Committee meeting on population. There is an emerging consensus among national Governments and donor agencies regarding the need for a mechanism for coordinating all international assistance in the field of population. In some cases, the lack of coordination of project activities has not only hindered the design and fulfilment of population policies at national and local levels but also duplicated programme efforts and wasted resources. The growing realization that collaboration and coordination at both national and international levels could play a critical role in strengthening national capability in managing population policies and programmes has encouraged some agencies to coordinate their programme efforts with those of Governments and other donors. To facilitate and enhance efforts in this direction, Governments and agencies would need to stipulate clearly the terms and conditions for assistance adapted to each country's situation and resources.

376. In their efforts to achieve self-reliance in mobilizing and managing resources for population programmes, Governments have increasingly been focusing their attention on such management efficiency issues as decentralization and accountability. The decentralization of the delivery of services for population programmes and the participation of local communities and non-governmental and private-sector organizations in all population areas have been gaining momentum. Additionally, many national and local institutions have demonstrated that they can be efficient executing agents in cost-sharing and cost-recovery schemes, particularly when they have reliable accounting, recording, reporting and auditing systems, together with strong managerial capabilities.

377. Experience over the past two decades with regard to family planning programmes has shown that good quality service, with sound management support systems and innovative public education efforts, could produce very rapid changes in reproductive behaviour in different socio-economic and cultural settings. In addition, there is growing realization of the urgent need to extend quality services to underserved areas, since people will use them if they are available. In their efforts to combine easy access, privacy and high-quality services and products with affordability, developing countries have tried a number of initiatives. Some of the most successful recent ones include community-based distribution and social marketing programmes. Currently, contraceptive social marketing programmes are in place in many developing countries, and some have achieved complete self-sufficiency.

378.   The growing relative scarcity of financial resources for population programmes in developing countries has given rise to the implementation of more market-oriented strategies for contraceptive mix, service quality and cost-recovery, all aimed at cutting costs. There is agreement that closer coordination between health and family planning services and giving higher priority to the strengthening of family planning services within existing health facilities could contribute to more cost-effective and efficient use of scarce financial and human resources. Increasingly, family planning is being coupled with maternal and child health services and even with primary health-care packages. Other efficient measures include linking family planning to agricultural extension programmes, industrial work settings, social work programmes and community participation.

379.   The current review of the level of implementation of the Plan of Action indicates that, although the goal of population and development assistance is to foster self-reliance and although approximately two thirds of the costs of basic population programmes are covered by the developing countries themselves, it is important to recognize that in economically strapped developing countries the risk of project activities coming to a halt upon cessation of external funding is great. Without external assistance, some Governments can barely continue—much less expand—population programmes. Moreover, attempts in most countries to redefine the role of the State by transferring Government-owned enterprises to the private sector and the decentralization of decision-making are factors that could continue to affect the thrust and direction of population policies and programmes and, concomitantly, their sustainability and self-sufficiency.

380.   National self-reliance, the ultimate objective of technical assistance, demands that in the long run, both the financial and the human resources required for population programmes should come from domestic resources. There is no simple formula that applies equally to every country. However, the following elements need to be present: strong political commitment; strategic planning; and strong institutional and, in particular, managerial capabilities to plan, implement and coordinate population programmes. The involvement of women in all stages of planning and execution of programmes is also fundamental. Increasingly, there is recognition of the need not only to meet the existing demand for family planning but also to increase it by reaching hitherto relatively neglected groups, especially teenagers and men. Experience has shown that efforts to meet existing demand with sensitive and varied programmes have helped to create new demand. In keeping with this recognition, Governments should set clear population objectives, establish targets and plans, and ensure that adequate budgetary allocations are made for reproductive health programmes, including family planning and complementary socio-economic programmes that are in accord with those objectives. Governments should also direct their efforts to generating and mobilizing domestic resources in order to implement such objectives in an efficient and timely manner.

381.   The Programme of Action lists a series of specific steps that Governments could take to facilitate the retention and effective deployment of programme personnel. It recommends giving special consideration to the basic

education, training, employment and equal pay of women at all levels; the inclusion of both women and youth in the development and maintenance of databases of national experts and institutions of excellence; and ensuring effective communication with, and the involvement of, programme beneficiaries at all levels. The Programme of Action further specifies the type of data needed for client-centred management information systems for population and development—data on clientele, expenditures, infrastructure, service accessibility, output and quality of services.

NOTES

[1]"Kilimanjaro Programme of Action for African Population and Self-reliant Development" (E/ECA/CM. 10/14, annex II). The document was adopted by the Second African Population Conference and endorsed by the Economic Commission for Africa, at its nineteenth session, held from 26 to 30 April 1984. The Kilimanjaro Programme of Action was the African contribution to the International Conference on Population (see E/CONF.76/6, annex V).

[2]See the Denpasar Declaration on Population and Development, adopted at the Ministerial Meeting on Population of the Non-Aligned Movement, Bali, 9-13 November 1993 (A/48/746, annex III).

XIII. INTERNATIONAL COOPERATION

382.   International cooperation is increasingly perceived as essential to the achievement of long-term planetary security. The modern expression "technical cooperation" has almost completely replaced the old term "technical assistance". This has been the result of recognizing that development activities need the participation of many actors on an equal footing, with the recipient country, the donor community and the provider of technical assistance perceived as partners in the same enterprise. Technical cooperation and financial assistance have played a crucial role in promoting and supporting population programmes in the developing countries, and the Plan of Action recognizes this role in achieving its goals and objectives (para. 100). The Plan of Action also invites countries to share their experiences and urges developed countries to increase their assistance to developing countries and the United Nations system in order to ensure a proper response to the issues raised in the Plan of Action (paras. 101, 102 and 104). The present chapter concentrates on two particular issues: priority areas for technical cooperation, and the strengthening of the population programme of the United Nations system.

Issue No. 28.   Priority areas for international cooperation

383.   The preceding sections of the present report have illustrated some of the many positive developments that have taken place since the adoption of the World Population Plan of Action in 1974. Many of those developments have been possible because of the recognition accorded to population as an important sector of international cooperation by national Governments and the international community. Developing countries have made significant progress in formulating population policies and programmes. However, economic recession, rising debt burdens and misplaced priorities, occurring simultaneously with those remarkable achievements, have limited, and in many countries reduced, the availability of funds hitherto programmed for population activities. During the period under review, the need for technical cooperation in population increased significantly. Although the amount of financial assistance has grown over the years, the gap between needs and resources has not been reduced significantly.

Priorities according to the Plan of Action

384.   The Plan of Action offers a series of recommendations, such as respect of national sovereignty, the value of sharing mutual experiences, the need to increase assistance to developing countries, and the role to be played by the United Nations system and by non-governmental organizations. It singles out the area of training in the field of population for special attention (paras. 100-106). Mexico City recommendation 81, building upon the provisions of the Plan of Action, is more specific and places special emphasis on a

128

number of areas such as the integration of population factors into development planning; improvement of the status and participation of women; collection and analysis of data; biomedical and social research; identification of successful programmes and dissemination of such findings; and implementation of monitoring, evaluation systems and training.

385. The Economic and Social Council studied the findings of the third review and appraisal of the Plan of Action in 1989 and recommended that the Governments concerned and the international community give the highest priority to assisting the population programmes of the least developed countries with large populations and high rates of population growth, in particular those in sub-Saharan Africa (resolution 1989/92, annex).

Priorities according to national Governments

386. Information from the Population Policy Data Bank indicates that an overwhelming majority—nine out of 10 developing countries—consider that they will need the support of international technical cooperation at least for another decade. The programme areas that have been identified by Governments as of the highest priority are information on population dynamics, followed by population policy formulation, data collection and processing, and family planning programmes. In spite of the high level of concern expressed by Governments on many occasions on issues related to population redistribution, technical cooperation programmes on these issues have been signalled as having the lowest priority or no priority at all.[1] Undependable funding, reduced levels of funding, and slowness in implementation have been identified by the Governments of countries receiving financial assistance as the two major difficulties confronted.

387. With respect to the priorities given to the different, specific components of current and future technical cooperation, national Governments have given the highest preference for computer equipment and software and for in-service and short-term training programmes. The lowest priority has been given to the provision of resident experts.

388. In relation to technical cooperation programmes among developing countries, the experience during the period under consideration has been limited, particularly because of the lack of available resources. Nevertheless, many Governments have indicated that in the field of population, such technical cooperation has an important potential for fostering a stronger political commitment to the solution of population issues and facilitating the exchange of similar experiences under similar conditions.

Priorities according to the multilateral organizations

389. Financial assistance for technical cooperation activities in the field of population flows from the donor community (Governments from developed countries and private sources, principally foundations) to the recipients (developing countries and national non-governmental organizations) through three major channels: bilateral, multilateral and private sector. According to information on expenditures for population assistance compiled by UNFPA (which includes data from 17 donor countries which are members of the

(OECD) Development Assistance Committee, nine multilateral organizations of the United Nations system and 37 international non-governmental organizations), in 1991 there were 141 countries that benefited from financial population assistance. During the same year, those 141 countries expended US$ 732 million (39 per cent was channelled through bilateral, 34 per cent through multilateral and 27 per cent through non-governmental organizations) (UNFPA, 1993). Data from table 15 indicate an absolute increase in funds during the period 1982-1991, a proportional increase in bilateral funds, a relative decline in multilateral funds and relative proportional stability of non-governmental resources. In considering those figures, it should be borne in mind that many activities included in the Plan of Action and receiving the support of the international community are not classified as population assistance but appear under other labels. This is the case, for example, with technical cooperation to reduce mortality, which usually appears as health assistance.

390. According to the same source of information, during the period 1982-1991, the commitments made by donor countries to the field of population assistance rose from 1.12 per cent of their official development assistance in 1982 to 1.34 per cent in 1991 (the highest value during the period 1982-1991, although the corresponding figure in the early 1970s was 2 per cent). The corresponding values of those commitments as a proportion of gross national product devoted to population assistance were 0.0071 and 0.0092 per cent respectively. Such assistance represented US$ 0.18 per capita in 1991, as compared with US$ 0.134 per capita in 1982 (both figures in constant 1985 United States dollars) (UNFPA, 1993).

391. It is very difficult to find complete information on the distribution of commitments or expenditures by programme area for all sources or channels of financial assistance. In 1985, UNFPA started a biannual compilation of such data for all sources of population assistance. Table 16 presents the amount of donor expenditures by programme area, using the Standard Classification of Population Activities that has been adopted by ACC and employed by UNFPA since 1976. Table 17 shows UNFPA expenditures by programme distribution; the figures are part of total donor expenditures. The distribution by programme area provides an indication of the priorities established by UNFPA and the donor community. In both cases, family planning activities accounted for a high proportion of population assistance (with a tendency towards increase among the total donor community during the period under consideration); communication and education accounted for the second highest proportion in 1991, reflecting a trend towards expansion. The proportion of assistance for basic data collection, on the other hand, tended to decrease proportionally during the period, particularly at UNFPA. The trend was due to increased national investment in this area and the dependence of such expenditures on the cycles of census activity.

392. UNFPA was directed by the UNDP Governing Council to allocate 80 per cent of its annual country programme resources to priority countries by 1994. Priority countries qualify for priority status if they first meet a gross national product per capita requirement, then fall within established threshold levels for two of the following five criteria: absolute annual population increase; infant mortality; fertility; female literacy; and agricultural population

TABLE 15. EXPENDITURES FOR POPULATION ASSISTANCE, BY CHANNEL OF DISTRIBUTION, 1982-1991[a]

Channel of distribution	1982	1983	1984	1985	1986	1987	1988	1989	1990	1991
	Thousands of current United States dollars									
Bilateral..............	101 587	98 565	134 383	161 406	129 336	145 297	163 330	208 437	231 325	286 487
	Percentage of total									
	28	28	32	34	36	36	29	40	38	39
	Thousands of current United States dollars									
Multilateral[b]	153 897	153 267	171 878	182 641	105 070	112 129	161 755	142 822	169 646	249 376
	Percentage of total									
	42	43	40	39	30	28	29	28	28	34
	Thousands of current United States dollars									
Non-governmental organizations..........	111 761	100 933	118 936	125 170	121 022	149 813	242 029	165 813	200 822	196 022
	Percentage of total									
	30	29	28	27	34	37	43	32	33	27
	Thousands of current United States dollars									
Total[c]	367 246	352 766	425 198	469 216	355 427	407 241	567 113	517 072	601 794	731 885

Source: UNFPA, *Global Population Assistance Report, 1982-1991* (New York, 1993), p. 18, table 4.

[a]The administrative costs entailed in the provision of assistance were not ascertained and may or may not be included in the expenditure figures shown.

[b]The multilateral category does not include the World Bank, since the Bank's expenditure data for population activities were not available to the survey.

[c]Figures may not add up to totals, and percentages may not add up to 100, owing to rounding.

131

TABLE 16. TOTAL DONOR EXPENDITURES, BY PROGRAMME AREA, 1982-1990
(Percentage)

Programme area	1982	1985	1989	1990
Basic data collection.............................	6.1	2.9	5.1	4.1
Population dynamics.............................	5.3	4.6	5.3	5.8
Policy formulation/evaluation	3.1	3.0	3.3	4.9
Policy implementation........................	0.3	0.4	0.5	0.1
Family planning programmes...............	59.3	64.0	69.7	59.5
Communication and education............	5.4	6.5	13.2	14.5
Special programmes	1.2	1.2	1.6	3.2
Multisector...	5.8	5.0	0.3	6.3
Not specified......................................	13.5	12.4	1.0	1.7
Total	100.0	100.0	100.0	100.0
		Total expenditure in millions of United States dollars		
	376.7	483.2	510.3	590.1

Sources: UNFPA, Global Population Assistance Report, 1982-1985 (New York, 1988), table 5; Global Population Assistance Report, 1982-1989 (New York, 1991), table A; and unpublished data provided by UNFPA.

TABLE 17. UNFPA EXPENDITURES, BY PROGRAMME AREA, 1975-1991
(Percentage)

Programme area	1975	1982	1985	1989	1991
Basic data collection.............................	20.1	17.3	7.5	11.6	9.1
Population dynamics.............................	5.9	12.0	11.0	12.9	11.7
Policy formulation/evaluation	4.7	6.9	6.1	7.7	9.2
Policy implementation........................	0.0	0.8	0.5	0.1	0.1
Family planning programmes...............	48.3	39.9	50.4	44.7	43.7
Communication and education............	11.0	10.9	13.4	16.9	17.0
Special programmes	2.1	1.2	1.1	3.6	6.0
Multisector...	7.9	11.0	10.0	2.5	3.1
Total	100.0	100.0	100.0	100.0	100.0
			Total expenditure in millions of United States dollars		
	61.4	104.9	128.2	157.4	171.8

Sources: Report on the Monitoring of Multilateral Population Assistance (New York, UNFPA, 1989), table 4; and UNFPA annual reports for 1990 and 1992.

per hectare of arable land. This ensures that UNFPA concentrates its assistance on activities in countries most in need of support. This strategy also assures that UNFPA support to national programmes is consistent over time yet flexible enough to meet changing population programme needs, which are assessed by UNFPA with independence from external political considerations.

393. It is important to acknowledge again some of the major achievements in the field of technical cooperation during the past two decades. Among them was the recognition, in the donor community and Governments in the developing countries, that population was an important component of the development equation and that technical cooperation was a key complement to national efforts, but never a substitute for them. The donor community has

been respectful of the sovereign right of countries to define their national population programmes, and the neutrality exhibited by multilateral assistance has been highly appreciated by developing countries. Technical cooperation activities have been better employed by countries having a strong political commitment and institutional support, including the competence to coordinate such assistance, and the appropriate provision of local human and budgetary resources. Many examples illustrate that technical cooperation was rendered more productive when national Governments worked in strong partnership with the private sector, community organizations and other grass-roots nongovernmental organizations.

394. To meet future needs, just in the area of human reproduction, additional resources are required for expanding services to respond to the unmet demand for family planning, particularly for creating the social and economic conditions that are most conducive to reducing the demand for additional children. However, it is also essential for those resources to be used effectively. Adequately estimating resource requirements and planning their effective utilization require accounting for a variety of programme elements, in terms of what they will contribute to the satisfaction of unmet needs and what they will cost. It is important to take into account that the future expansion of services should satisfy both current unmet needs and the future demand generated by an improvement in the quality of current services and the adoption of better strategies. Indeed, the pressures of increased numbers to be served, combined with the budget squeezes in which many developing countries now find themselves, could erode service quality and further swell the pool of the underserved.

395. Future technical cooperation is crucial for achieving the population goals and objectives agreed upon by the international community. Increased funding, based on careful assessments of resource requirements, is fundamental. It is currently estimated that international assistance would be needed to cover about one third of the total cost of the major components of population programmes in the developing countries. The Amsterdam Declaration of 1989 called for a doubling in the level of annual global funding of population and reproductive health programmes in the developing countries, from US$ 4.5 billion to US$ 9 billion by the end of the 1990s. Some progress has been made in moving towards this goal, but it is still far from clear that it will be reached.

396. In the context of the preparatory activities for the International Conference on Population and Development, it has been estimated that the total annual cost of four basic packages of population activities would be (in 1993 United States dollars) US$ 17.0 billion in the year 2000 and US$ 21.7 billion in 2015, broken down as follows:

(a) A core package composed of family planning commodities and service delivery; many components of primary health care and maternal and child health; information, education and communication activities; family planning training; and management information activities. Cost: US$ 10.2 billion in the year 2000 and US$ 13.8 billion in 2015;

(*b*)   An expanded package for reproductive health care going beyond the usual components of family planning programmes but still feasible in the context of primary health care: education and services for prenatal care, normal delivery and postnatal care; prevention and treatment of reproductive health conditions, including infertility; information, education and counselling on human sexuality, sexual and reproductive health, and responsible parenthood; and referral of sexually transmitted diseases and HIV/AIDS. Cost: US$ 5.0 billion in the year 2000 and US$ 6.1 billion in 2015;

(*c*)   A third package of activities for the prevention of sexually transmitted diseases (including HIV infection), consisting of mass media and school education programmes and expanded condom distribution. Cost: US$ 1.3 billion in the year 2000 and US$ 1.5 billion in 2015;

(*d*)   A fourth package of activities that include population data collection, analysis and dissemination, and policy formulation. Cost: US$ 220 million to 700 million per annum (depending on the decennial population census cycle).

397.   The Programme of Action stresses that at the programme level, national capacity-building for population and development and transfer of appropriate technology and know-how to developing countries and countries with economies in transition must be core objectives and central activities for international cooperation. It indicates that in this respect, it is important to find accessible ways to meet the large commodity needs of family planning programmes through the local production of contraceptives of assured quality and affordability, for which technology cooperation, joint ventures and other forms of technical assistance should be encouraged.

398.   In addition, the Programme of Action recommends that Governments should ensure that national development plans take note of anticipated international funding and cooperation in their population and development programmes, including loans from international financial institutions, particularly with respect to national capacity-building, technology cooperation and transfer of appropriate technology. It specifies that, in turn, those loans should be provided on favourable terms, including on concessional and preferential terms, as mutually agreed, and that technology cooperation and transfer should take into account the need to protect international property rights and the special needs of developing countries.

399.   Furthermore, the Programme of Action recommends that recipient Governments should strengthen their national coordination mechanisms for international cooperation in population and development. In consultation with donors, recipient Governments should also clarify the responsibilities assigned to various types of development partners, including intergovernmental and international non-governmental organizations, based on careful consideration of their comparative advantages in the context of national development priorities and of their ability to interact with national development partners. In turn, the international community should assist recipient Governments in undertaking those coordinating efforts.

400.   Beyond the World Population Plan of Action and the recommendations for its further implementation, the Programme of Action adopted at

Cairo specifies the resource figures needed to achieve the objectives and quantitative goals in population and development. In addition, it puts forward a crucially urgent challenge to the international community to strive towards the fulfilment of its agreed targets for support. It also invites donor organizations to coordinate their financing policies and planning procedures in order to improve the impact, complementarity and cost-effectiveness of their contributions. It also insists on ensuring that international assistance for population and development activities is used effectively in meeting national population and development objectives, and it addresses the issue of accountability.

401. In devising an appropriate balance between funding sources, the Programme of Action stresses that more attention be given to South/South cooperation and to new ways of mobilizing private contributions, particularly in partnership with non-governmental organizations. It recommends that the international community should urge donor agencies to improve and modify their funding procedures in order to facilitate and give higher priority to supporting direct South-South collaborative arrangements.

402. The Programme of Action also specifies the criteria for the allocation of external financial resources in developing countries. In addition, it indicates that countries with economies in transition should receive temporary assistance for population and development activities in the light of the difficult economic and social problems those countries face at present.

403. Finally, the Programme of Action suggests that innovative financing, including new ways of generating public and private financing resources and various forms of debt relief, should be explored. Similarly, it encourages international financial assistance, particularly in population and reproductive health, including family planning and sexual health care.

*Issue No. 29. Strengthening the population programme
of the United Nations system*

404. Since its inception, the United Nations has been involved in a variety of population activities. During the past two decades, more than 20 units, bodies and organizations of the United Nations system have been carrying out activities that include, *inter alia*, data collection, research and analysis, dissemination of information, training, provision of technical cooperation and financial assistance, and monitoring and evaluation of projects and programmes. Such activities are coordinated by the Economic and Social Council, and for that purpose, the Council is advised by the Population Commission. The Population Commission was established in 1946, and its terms of reference remained almost unchanged until the 1974 World Population Conference, when the Council requested the Commission to examine on a biennial basis the implementation of the Plan of Action and to contribute to its quinquennial review and appraisal. After the 1984 International Conference on Population, the Council reaffirmed the role of the Commission as the principal intergovernmental body to arrange for studies and advise the Council on population matters.[2]

405. Within the Department for Economic and Social Information and Policy Analysis of the United Nations Secretariat there are two important units: the Population Division, and the Statistical Division. The Population Division, which is the technical secretariat of the Population Commission, is in charge of monitoring world population trends and policies through the study of mortality, fertility, internal and international migration and urbanization, and other demographic phenomena, and of coordinating the quinquennial review and appraisal of the progress made in achieving the goals and objectives of the Plan of Action. It also estimates and projects population size and structure, examines the relationships between population change, resources, the environment and socio-economic development, participates in technical cooperation activities, and houses the coordinating unit of the global Population Information Network (POPIN), mentioned in paragraph 243 above. The Statistical Division, which is the technical secretariat of the Statistical Commission, collects, compiles and disseminates demographic and related statistics produced by Governments; it engages in the research and development of methods of data collection on population and housing censuses, civil registration and vital statistics, and household surveys, and promotes the development of demographic statistical databases for population and development analysis; it also prepares handbooks and technical studies and participates in technical cooperation activities.

406. A trust fund for population activities was established by the Secretary-General in July 1967; two years later, it was renamed the United Nations Fund for Population Activities (UNFPA) and was put under the administration of UNDP. Renamed the United Nations Population Fund in 1987 while retaining the abbreviation UNFPA (Economic and Social Council resolution 1987/175 and General Assembly resolution 42/430), the Fund at present supports population programmes in 137 countries and territories and has field offices, each headed by a country director, in 58 of them. Assistance at the country level is being provided, in most cases, as part of a country programme that defines the objectives and strategy for UNFPA assistance in the framework of national population and development objectives. Those country programmes, which used to be based on "needs assessment" exercises, have been developed since 1988 on the basis of programme review and strategy development exercises. UNFPA also funds regional and interregional activities and services that supplement and complement activities at the country level. For example, the Fund extends technical assistance and advisory services to country programmes through its recently established Country Support Teams system, which became operational in 1992. The system comprises eight multidisciplinary teams located in the developing regions. Participating in it are the Department for Economic and Social Information and Policy Analysis of the United Nations Secretariat, the regional commissions, ILO, FAO, UNESCO, WHO and non-governmental organizations.

407. Each of the five regional commissions has a population unit whose programme of work includes research and analysis, dissemination of information and, in some cases, also technical cooperation. The specific contents

of their programmes of work vary according to the characteristics of each region and are supervised by the corresponding regional intergovernmental body. Some of the regions have adopted regional programmes or plans of action that are reviewed every 10 years and may be conceived as the regional variants of the World Population Plan of Action.

408. Other programmes and bodies of the United Nations include population-related activities in their programmes of work. The United Nations Centre for Human Settlements (Habitat) assists countries in some actions that have implications for the distribution of population over the territory concerned. UNICEF cooperates with countries in their activities pertaining to the protection of children and participates in family planning actions that are part of maternal and child health programmes. The United Nations Conference on Trade and Development (UNCTAD) includes in its programme of work activities related to the situation of migrant workers and other population matters related to international trade. UNEP has been involved in research and analysis on the relationships between population, resources and the environment. After the 1992 United Nations Conference on Environment and Development, UNEP and the Department for Policy Coordination and Sustainable Development of the United Nations Secretariat planned to strengthen their efforts in this area. UNHCR is in charge of providing protection to refugees, finding durable solutions to their problems and dispensing assistance towards self-sufficiency and emergency relief. Finally, the World Food Programme (WFP), in addition to its many activities that have a clear impact on morbidity and mortality levels, has many programmes that include components affecting fertility or migration patterns.

409. Some of the specialized agencies undertake population activities, and their work is coordinated by the Economic and Social Council. Their activities include, in general, research and analysis, technical cooperation, and the dissemination of information. The ILO conducts research on the demographic aspects of employment and social security, provides information on family planning and other population-related matters, and assists Governments in formulating/implementing their population policies and in establishing their population units. FAO provides advice and technical assistance to countries on matters related to rural populations; its programme of work also includes research and analysis and population education and communication aimed at creating awareness. UNESCO concentrates on the creation of awareness about population issues and assists countries in their population information, education and communication programmes. WHO assists countries in the provision of family planning within maternal and child health-care systems, education and training for health workers, research and training in human reproduction, development of technologies in maternal and child health care, and the promotion of breast-feeding and the use of appropriate weaning foods and nutrition programmes. The United Nations Industrial Development Organization (UNIDO) has, in its programme of work related to population, activities such as the local production of contraceptives. Finally, the World Bank provides financial assistance in the field of population, directly or through its concessional lending affiliate, the International Development Association (IDA), in the form of credits and loans to borrowers. The Bank also conducts

research in and analysis of population and economic conditions at the global level and in those developing countries in which population and development are matters of concern.

Coordination

410. There are various mechanisms that ensure the harmonization, co-operation and coordination of population activities within the United Nations system. The Committee for Programme and Coordination (CPC), a standing committee of the Economic and Social Council and the principal subsidiary body dealing with matters related to planning, programming and coordination, assists both the Council and the General Assembly in their sector-by-sector examination of the programme of work of the United Nations, to guarantee the harmonization and complementarity of the different activities. CPC also proposes guidelines and recommends actions to appropriate units and organizations on their programmes of work and carries out assessments of legislative decisions on matters pertaining to coordination of activities. Population is one of the topics that has been included in the programme of work of CPC. After the 1984 International Conference on Population (Mexico City), it was agreed that relevant portions of the report of the UNDP Governing Council (the body then overseeing UNFPA's programme) should be made available to the Population Commission and vice versa.

411. ACC was established in 1947 as an inter-agency structure to ensure harmonization, cooperation and coordination within the United Nations system. It is composed of the executive heads of the agencies, programmes and organs of the system and is chaired by the Secretary-General himself. An ACC Subcommittee on Population functioned between 1968 and 1977 as an inter-agency coordinating entity but was abolished in 1977, as a result of the restructuring of the social and economic sectors of the United Nations system. Nevertheless, in 1979 ACC established the Ad Hoc Inter-agency Working Group on Demographic Estimates and Projections. ACC established ad hoc task forces for the 1984 and 1994 population conferences, as part of the preparatory work for those conferences.

412. In addition to the safe motherhood initiative mentioned in issue No. 14 above, other important coordinating mechanisms in the field of population include the Inter-Agency Consultative Committee (IACC), which was established by UNFPA in 1970 to discuss the Fund's programmes, policies, procedures and coordination issues; and the Joint Consultative Group on Policy (JCGP), which was established in 1981 by the executive heads of UNICEF, UNDP, UNFPA and WFP, to promote the consideration of child survival, family planning and the needs of vulnerable groups in their programmes of work. JCGP has been very active in other areas such as women and development, structural adjustment, training of personnel, and programme collaboration and coordination in Africa (including the sharing of common premises and services).

413. Population has been recognized as one of the fields in which the United Nations has been successful. In spite of the controversial character of population issues, the United Nations has served as a forum for open debate

and the negotiation of common strategies. Through its programme of research and analysis, it has accomplished pioneering work in the development of new methodologies for demographic data collection, demographic analysis, and, particularly, in creating awareness of the key role that population variables play in social and economic development. Its activities in technical cooperation and financial assistance have been appreciated by developing countries because of the neutral character of multilateral assistance and the high quality of the services provided. Population is one area where effective coordination has been demonstrated within the United Nations system. Since the role of the United Nations in the field of population has been recognized by the international community and the public in general and because of the growing interest of countries in this area, the population programme of the United Nations needs to be strengthened.

414. Besides guiding the work programme of the Population Division, the Commission on Population and Development receives periodic reports on the activities of the United Nations system (including the World Bank), UNFPA and intergovernmental and non-governmental organizations. Furthermore, at every session of the Commission, representatives of the Statistics Division, the regional commissions, United Nations programmes and bodies, and the specialized agencies make statements on their organization's activities. This de facto arrangement has facilitated the work of the Economic and Social Council with respect to its coordination function within the system, although *de jure* the Commission does not have such a mandate. Therefore, the strengthening of the population programme of the United Nations also requires the strengthening of the corresponding intergovernmental machinery.

NOTES

[1]This information refers to the aggregate situation of the group of developing countries. The countries in the ECLAC region usually give a higher priority to cooperation in the field of population redistribution than countries in other regions.

[2]Economic and Social Council resolution 1985/4 of 28 May 1985, para. 1. See also Council resolutions 3 (III) of 3 October 1946 and 150 (VII) of 10 August 1948, and decisions 87 (LVIII) and 89 (LVIII) of 6 May 1975.

XIV. PARTNERSHIP WITH NON-GOVERNMENTAL SECTORS

415. It is widely recognized that many of the socio-economic issues that are part of the work programme of the United Nations at present were covered in the pioneering activities of non-governmental organizations before the United Nations decided to confront them. Non-governmental organizations have been established on a voluntary basis by individuals or groups interested in a particular issue. Their purposes are diverse: some are professional associations (for example, of public health workers); others are groups consisting of a particular segment of the population (for example, the elderly and women); others are affiliate members of a specific religion or political orientation; some are interested in a particular humanitarian cause; and others are organizations devoted to teaching, conducting research or disseminating information.

416. Non-governmental organizations can be local, national or international, or they can belong to the profit-oriented private sector. Those having an international status may have national or local affiliates, but the majority of them carry out their activities within the boundaries of their country. Those in the private sector, including national and transnational corporations and their representative associations, play a valuable role in the social and economic development of the world. In many instances, they have the capability and capacity to produce and deliver goods and services in an efficient manner. They are able to use available communications facilities to conduct a dialogue with their staff and the public and to take voluntary initiatives in the social sphere. The Charter of the United Nations (Article 71) deems that the Economic and Social Council may make suitable arrangements for consultation with non-governmental organizations that are concerned with matters within its competence. For this purpose, the Council has established a series of mechanisms and procedures for the granting of consultative status to such organizations (resolution 1296 (XLIV)). In this task, the Council is assisted by the Committee on Non-Governmental Organizations.

Issue No. 30. Strengthening the partnership with non-governmental sectors

417. In the field of population, many non-governmental organizations were conducting research, creating awareness and providing services well in advance of many Governments and intergovernmental organizations. On many occasions, once national Governments had decided to act in a particular field, non-governmental organizations worked in partnership with the public sector in the delivery of services and implementation of programmes. Such collaboration has been instrumental in ensuring that national policy goals are achieved. Non-governmental organizations have also acted as catalysts for change,

often serving as a voice for previously unrecognized concerns, reaching underserved groups, setting quality standards more responsive to the needs of beneficiaries, and developing innovative and cost-effective approaches.

418. Many of the non-governmental organizations that participate in the work of the United Nations have an international character and are not-for-profit. Nevertheless, in the field of population, at both the international and particularly the national levels, there is a substantial number of for-profit organizations that have contributed greatly to the understanding of population issues and to the implementation of programmes, through contract work performed for governmental agencies and for other non-governmental organizations and for the United Nations system. In many countries, population activities have benefited from the strengthening of the private, profit-oriented sector, which in many cases contributes to the development of local financial, managerial and technological capacity for the production and distribution of commodities and services in an effective and cost-efficient manner. In such instances, an increasing number of Governments are tending to rely more on the effectiveness of the private sector, thus creating new forms of partnership.

419. Local community organizations are also receiving increased attention. Some of them have been created by the public sector, while others came into existence by the will of the communities themselves. In terms of their character, they exhibit a wide range, extending from simple kinship structures to more complex political, social, economic, religious and educational groups. Because their existence usually transcends the short life duration of other types of organizations, for local communities, particularly those that are isolated from the mainstream of national life, they are an important (if not the only) source of social cohesion, providing support to the needs of families and individuals. Finally, considering their proximity to the grass roots of society, local community organizations are an important link with local governments and other non-governmental organizations, thus forming part of the network that constitutes the fabric of society.

420. The significant financial contribution of non-governmental organizations to population activities is another illustration of their particular interest in this area. Data presented in table 15 indicate that during the period 1982-1991, of the total expenditures for population assistance (US$ 1,532.3 million), one third was channelled through international non-governmental organizations, of which about US$ 400 million (26 per cent) was committed directly by the non-governmental organizations themselves (UNFPA, 1993). Such figures constitute just a small visible part of the iceberg, because they refer only to international non-governmental organizations: If the contribution made by national, and particularly local, non-governmental organizations were added to those figures, the total would be significantly higher.

421. Taking into account the mutual benefits obtained from the closer collaboration between non-governmental organizations and the United Nations, as a follow-up to the International Conference on Population, the Economic and Social Council requested the Secretary-General to prepare periodic reports on the work of intergovernmental and non-governmental

organizations in the implementation of the World Population Plan of Action. To date, four such reports have been prepared, covering an increasing number of organizations and providing the Population Commission and the Council with valuable information on the characteristics and scope of the organizations, their human and financial resources, and their areas of work.

422. The report of the Secretary-General on the work of intergovernmental and non-governmental organizations in the implementation of the World Population Plan of Action (E/CN.9/1994/7), prepared for submission to the Population Commission at its twenty-seventh session (March 1994), includes a listing of 135 international non-governmental organizations that carry out important population activities; close to half of them are not in consultative status with the Economic and Social Council, either because they have not applied for such status or because they are for-profit organizations, although their activities are very close to the goals of the Plan of Action. Among the organizations that should be mentioned because of their significant contribution to the population field are:

(a) The International Planned Parenthood Federation, which was established in 1952, is the largest international private voluntary organization. It affiliates independent family planning associations in over 135 countries;

(b) The Population Council, also created in 1952, is involved in biomedical research in the field of human reproduction, social science research, and technical cooperation in family planning and other population-related programmes;

(c) The International Union for the Scientific Study of Population, which was established in 1924 and is the leading international professional association for individuals in the field of population. It groups close to 2,000 professionals from 124 different countries.

423. Recognizing the pioneering role and the important contribution of non-governmental organizations, the Plan of Action invited them to collaborate in the implementation of the Plan of Action and urged Governments to utilize fully the support of intergovernmental and non-governmental organizations (para. 96). The International Conference on Population not only recognized and commended the contributions of non-governmental organizations but also emphasized the involvement of those organizations. Mexico City recommendation 84 urged Governments to encourage the innovative activities of non-governmental organizations and to draw upon their expertise, experience and resources in implementing national programmes. Therefore, enhancing the partnership with non-governmental organizations will generate mutual benefits for local and national Governments, the United Nations and the non-governmental organizations themselves.

424. The key role of non-governmental organizations is emphasized throughout the text of the Programme of Action adopted at Cairo. In particular, Governments are urged to ensure the participation of women's organizations in the design and implementation of population and development programmes, given that involving women at all levels, especially the managerial level, is seen as critical to meeting the objectives of and implementing the Programme of Action.

425.   The Programme of Action also specifies what Governments, intergovernmental organizations and international financial institutions can do to strengthen the role of non-governmental organizations, without compromising their autonomy—for example, promote regular dialogue and consultations, appropriate training and outreach activities, and include representatives of non-governmental organizations on country delegations to regional and international forums where issues on population and development are discussed. The Programme of Action further indicates the steps that those same institutions need to take to ensure transparency, accountability and effective division of labour, such as making available to the non-governmental organizations necessary information and documents. In turn, non-governmental organizations and their networks and local communities are encouraged to strengthen their interaction with their constituencies, ensure the transparency of their activities, mobilize public opinion, participate in the implementation of population and development programmes, and actively contribute to the national, regional and international debate on population and development issues.

426.   For the first time in the history of population conferences, the Programme of Action outlines issues and approaches related to the role of the for-profit sector in the implementation of population and development programmes, including the production and delivery of quality contraceptive commodities and services with appropriate information and education, in a socially responsible, culturally sensitive, acceptable and cost-effective manner. In addition, the Programme of Action recommends cooperation between Governments, non-governmental and international organizations, and the private, for-profit sector. It also recommends that two priorities for non-profit and profit-oriented organizations and their networks should be to develop mechanisms for the exchange of ideas and experiences in the population and development fields and to share innovative approaches and research and development initiatives. Governments are strongly encouraged to set standards for service delivery and to review legal, regulatory and import policies to identify and eliminate those policies that unnecessarily prevent or restrict the greater involvement of the private sector in service delivery and in the efficient production of commodities for reproductive health. In addition, Governments are advised to encourage the private sector to meet its responsibilities regarding consumer information dissemination in a culturally appropriate manner. The Programme of Action recommends that the profit-oriented sector, in turn, should consider how it might better assist non-profit non-governmental organizations to play a wider role in society through the enhancement or creation of suitable mechanisms to channel financial and other appropriate support to non-governmental organizations and their associations.

427.   Finally, the Programme of Action acknowledges and supports the role of private-sector employers in devising and implementing special programmes that help meet their employees' needs to combine work and family responsibilities. Similarly, organized health-care providers and health insurers are asked to continue including family planning and reproductive health services in the package of health benefits they provide.

XV. MONITORING, REVIEW AND APPRAISAL

Issue No. 31. Monitoring, review and appraisal

Monitoring of population trends, policies and programmes

428. The World Population Plan of Action recommended that a monitoring of population trends and policies should be undertaken continuously as a specialized activity of the United Nations and be reviewed biennially by the appropriate bodies of the United Nations system (para. 107). Mexico City recommendation 88 added that monitoring of the multilateral population programmes of the United Nations system aimed at the further implementation of the World Population Plan of Action should be undertaken by the Secretary-General of the United Nations, through appropriate arrangements.[1] The present chapter discusses the monitoring of population trends, policies and programmes, and the mandate for the review and appraisal of the World Population Plan of Action.

429. The monitoring of population trends is an activity that has been undertaken continuously since the initiation of the population programme of the United Nations in 1946. The first United Nations Population Inquiry among Governments was carried out in 1963-1964, with 53 Governments and the Holy See responding on their perceptions and policies. The results were instrumental in triggering a series of actions that were initiated by the Population Commission (March 1965), endorsed by the Economic and Social Council (July 1965), and finally ratified by the General Assembly, authorizing, *inter alia*, the provision of assistance for national family planning programmes.[2] However, it was only after 1974 that the United Nations received the mandate to conduct the monitoring of trends and policies in a systematic manner.

430. Within the United Nations, the Population Division of the Department for Economic and Social Information and Policy Analysis of the United Nations Secretariat is responsible for conducting and reporting on the monitoring of population trends and policies biennially, in collaboration with other units, bodies and organizations of the United Nations system. The first in the series of monitoring reports was prepared and published in 1977 and succeeding reports, in 1979, 1981, 1983, 1987, 1989 and 1991. A concise version of the report is also prepared and published biennially. The report usually includes a wide range of information about basic population variables and the views and policies adopted by national Governments on such topics as population growth and size; mortality; fertility; urbanization; internal and international migration; and the main structural elements—namely, sex, age, labour-force participation, demographic dependency and groups of special social and economic importance. The report also includes information on the interrelationships between population and other areas of concern such as employment, women, food and nutrition, socio-economic development, and the environ-

ment. During recent bienniums, the report has also contained a more detailed treatment of a special topic such as key issues in fertility and mortality; population trends and policies among the least developed countries; age structure; and refugees. Major sources of information include the outcome of demographic assessments, demographic research and studies, the findings of the United Nations Population Inquiries among Governments (the seventh of which has just been completed), and other relevant information available in the Population Policy Data Bank maintained by the Population Division.

431. Ever since the United Nations received a mandate to participate in technical cooperation activities and provide financial assistance, a series of mechanisms have been established for the purpose of monitoring the multilateral population programmes of the system. The International Conference on Population requested the Secretary-General to undertake the monitoring of multilateral population programmes of the United Nations system aimed at the further implementation of the World Population Plan of Action. In his report on the follow-up to General Assembly resolution 39/228 (A/41/179-E/1986/18), the Secretary-General recommended that UNFPA continue to monitor the multilateral population programmes and projects that it funds. The first report on multilateral population assistance was prepared in 1989 (E/1989/12), the second in 1991 (E/CN.9/1991/8) and the third in 1994 (E/CN.9/1994/6).

432. Also, as a follow-up to the Mexico City recommendations, the Economic and Social Council requested the Secretary-General to submit periodic overviews of the activities of the United Nations system in the field of population and periodic reports on the activities of intergovernmental and non-governmental organizations in the implementation of the Plan of Action (Council resolutions 1985/4, 1986/7 and 1987/72).

433. With these reports, the United Nations governing bodies and national Governments have a general overview of the level of implementation of the Plan of Action. More exactly, the reports provide information on population trends and tendencies, governmental views on those trends, and activities that have been undertaken by Governments, the United Nations system, other intergovernmental organizations, and by non-governmental organizations. Information concerning bilateral assistance, as mentioned above, is periodically collected by UNFPA and by OECD.

Review and appraisal of the World Population Plan of Action

434. The Plan of Action also specifies that a comprehensive and thorough review and appraisal of progress made towards achieving the goals and recommendations of the Plan of Action should be undertaken every five years by the United Nations system and that the findings of such systematic evaluations should be considered by the Economic and Social Council with the object of making, whenever necessary, appropriate modifications of the goals and recommendations of the Plan of Action (para. 108). The International Conference on Population simply reiterated these provisions.

435. In accordance with the above provisions, the Population Division has had responsibility for coordinating the four assessments that have been

undertaken. The first (1979) was conducted with the assistance of an Ad Hoc Group of Experts on Review and Appraisal of the World Population Plan of Action; the findings of the Fourth Population Inquiry among Governments, along with information provided by the regional commissions, the specialized agencies and other United Nations bodies and organizations, contributed to the assessment, mainly through the aforementioned Subcommittee on Population of ACC. The results were presented to the Population Commission and the Economic and Social Council, and the Council approved the findings and adopted 16 recommendations for the further implementation of the Plan (resolution 1979/32).

436.   The Economic and Social Council decided that the 1984 population conference should be devoted to the discussion of selected issues of the highest priority, with the aim of contributing to the process of review and appraisal of the World Population Plan of Action and to its further implementation (resolution 1981/87). Inter-agency participation for preparing the report was provided through the ACC Ad Hoc Task Force for the Conference. The report was submitted to the Preparatory Committee for the Conference, and their comments were used to prepare a revised version that was presented to the International Conference on Population. Subsequently, on the basis of the deliberations held at the Conference, a final version was prepared (United Nations, 1984). The Conference produced 88 recommendations for the further implementation of the Plan of Action.

437.   The third assessment was produced in 1989. It concentrated on a set of 31 selected issues. For that assessment, inter-agency participation was provided by the former Consultative Committee on Substantive Questions (Programme Matters) of ACC. The results of the Sixth Population Inquiry among Governments and responses from intergovernmental and non-governmental organizations were important sources of information. The Economic and Social Council, as recommended by the Population Commission, approved the report and adopted the 13 recommendations (resolution 1989/92).

438.   From the above presentation, it follows that important progress has been made in the directions set forth in the Plan of Action. The findings of the present report invite the conclusion that the World Population Plan of Action is an international instrument that has served as a standard reference and continues to rest firmly on a global consensus. Although there are many reasons for such achievements, it is important to emphasize the benefits that have resulted from bringing together the political will of Governments and the scientific and professional skills of many units of the United Nations and of numerous academic centres and professional associations and other non-governmental organizations.[3]

NOTES

[1]In a footnote to recommendation 88, the Governments of Mexico and India stated that, while joining the consensus, they considered that it was not for the Secretary-General to keep the imple-

mentation of population programmes funded by multilateral assistance under review, since that was exclusively the prerogative of Governments. In that sense, the Secretary-General might only keep under review the use of the assistance provided by United Nations agencies.

[2]See the report of an ad hoc committee of experts to the Population Commission (E/CN.9/182), Economic and Social Council resolution 1084 (XXXIX) of 30 July 1965, and General Assembly resolution 2211 (XXI) of 17 December 1966.

[3]Economic and Social Council resolution 1989/92, annex, para. 2.

REFERENCES

South Commission (1990). *The Challenge to the South: The Report of the South Commission.* New York: Oxford University Press.

United Nations (1975). *Report of the United Nations World Population Conference, 1974, Bucharest, 19-30 August 1974.* Sales No. E.75.XIII.3.

_____(1976). *Report of the World Conference of the International Women's Year, Mexico City, 19 June-2 July 1975.* Sales No. E.76.IV. 1.

_____(1979). *Review and Appraisal of the World Population Plan of Action.* Sales No. E.79.XIII.7.

_____(1980). *Report of the World Conference of the United Nations Decade for Women: Equality, Development and Peace, Copenhagen, 14 to 30 July 1980..* Sales No. E.80.IV.3 and corrigendum.

_____(1982). *Report of the World Assembly on Ageing, Vienna, 26 July to 6 August 1982.* Sales No. E.82.I.16.

_____(1984). *Report of the International Conference on Population, 1984, Mexico City, 6-14 August 1984.* Sales No. E.84.XIII.8 and corrigenda, chap. I, sect. B (III and IV).

_____(1985). *Report of the World Conference to Review and Appraise the Achievements of the United Nations Decade for Women: Equality, Development and Peace, Nairobi, 15-26 July 1985.* Sales E.85.IV.10.

_____(1986). *Review and Appraisal of the World Population Plan of Action: 1984 Report.* Sales No. E.86.XIII.2.

_____(1989a). Population Commission: report on the twenty-fifth session (21 February-2 March 1989). *Official Records of the Economic and Social Council, 1989, Supplement No. 6.* E/1989/24-E/CN.9/l989/8, paras. 11-21.

_____(1989b). *Review and Appraisal of the World Population Plan of Action: 1989 Report.* Sales No. E.89.XIII.11.

_____(1990). *The World's Women, 1970-1990: Trends and Statistics.* Sales No. E.90.XVII.3.

_____(1991). *Population and Human Rights: Proceedings of the Expert Group Meeting on Population and Human Rights, Geneva, 3-6 April 1989.* Sales No. E.91.XIII.8.

_____(1992a). Priority themes: equality: elimination of de jure and de facto discrimination against women. Report of the Secretary-General. E/CN.6/1992/7, para. 5.

_____(1992b). *World Population Monitoring, 1991.* ST/ESA/SER.A/126. Sales No. E.92.XIII.2.

_____(1993a). Report of the ACC Ad Hoc Inter-Agency Meeting for the International Conference on Population and Development. ACC/1993/17, para. 10.

_____(1993b). *Report of the United Nations Conference on Environment and Development, Rio de Janeiro, 3-14 June 1992,* vol. I, *Resolutions Adopted by the Conference.* Sales No. E.93.I.8 and corrigendum, resolution 1, annex II.

_____(1993c). *Report of the World Conference on Human Rights, Vienna, 14-25 June 1993.* A/CONF.157/24, part I.

_____(1993d). Recommendations of the Expert Group Meeting on Population and Women, Gaborone, Botswana, 22-26 June 1992: report of the Secretary-General. E/CONF.84/PC/6.

_____(1993e). Recommendations of the Expert Group Meeting on Family Planning, Health and Family Well-being, Bangalore, India, 26-30 October 1992: report of the Secretary-General. E/CONF.84/PC/7.

_____(1993f). *Official Records of the General Assembly, Forty-seventh Session, Supplement No. 12A.* A/47/12.

_____(1994a). Report of the ACC Ad Hoc Task Force for the International Conference on Population and Development, 1994. ACC/1992/22, para. 17.

_____(1994b). Report of the International Conference on Population and Development (Cairo, 5-13 September 1994). A/CONF.171/13 and Add.l.

_____(1995a). *World Population Prospects: The 1994 Revision.* Sales No. E.95.XIII.16.

_____(1995b). *World Population Monitoring, 1993.* Sales No. E.95.XIII.8.

_____(1995c). *World Urbanization Prospects: The 1994 Revision.* Sales No. E.95.XIII.12.

_____, Economic Commission for Africa (1992). Report of the Third African Population Conference, Dakar, Senegal, 11-12 December 1992. E/CONF.84/PC/13, annex II.

United Nations Population Fund (1990). *Report of the International Forum on Population in the Twenty-first Century, Amsterdam, the Netherlands, 6-9 November 1989.* New York.

_____(1992). Future contraceptive requirements and logistics management needs. Paper presented at the Expert Group Meeting on Family Planning, Health and Family Well-being (Bangalore, 26-30 October 1992).

_____(1993). *Global Population Assistance Report, 1982-1991.* New York.

World Bank (1987). *Preventing the Tragedy of Maternal Deaths: Report on the International Safe Motherhood Conference, Nairobi, Kenya, February 1987.* Washington, D.C.

World Commission on Environment and Development (1987). *Our Common Future: The Report of the World Commission on Environment and Development.* Oxford and New York: Oxford University Press.

World Meteorological Organization (1992). *Report of the International Conference on Water and the Environment: Development Issues for the Twenty-first Century, 26-31 January 1992, Dublin, Ireland. The Dublin Statement and Report of the Conference.* Geneva.

Litho in United Nations, New York
95-93849—December 1995—4,785
ISBN 92-1-151299-9

United Nations publication
Sales No. E.95.XIII.27
ST/ESA/SER.A/152